Chinese Idioms
and
Their Stories

Written by Zhang Ciyun

Foreign Languages Press   Beijing

First edition   1996

Illustrated by   **Li Daimei**
                    Zhang Geming

Edited by   **Liu Mingzhen**

ISBN 7-119-01774-8

Copyright 1996 by Foreign Languages Press, Beijing, China

Published by Foreign Languages Press
24 Baiwanzhuang Road, Beijing 100037, China

Printed by Foreign Languages Printing House
19 Chegongzhuang Xilu, Beijing 100044, China

Distributed by China International Book Trading Corporation
35 Chegongzhuang Xilu, Beijing 100044, China
P.O. Box 399, Beijing, China

Printed in the People's Republic of China

Contents

Introduction

Whenever the "cat gets your tongue" or a situation demands meaning "in a nutshell," there can be no better way to "say it with words" than injecting an idiom into the conversation. The Chinese language is especially rich in idioms where a suitable phrase can be found for every occasion. The expression contained in idioms is intricately linked to each individual culture and, although they are refined methods of expressing a specific meaning, the richness of this form of language is greatly enhanced by an understanding of the historical background to the origin of the phrase. Chinese idioms abound in stories, many of which are now forgotten or unknown to modern society even though the idioms themselves are used every day.

Originally published in serial form in the *China Daily*, this collection of one hundred Chinese idioms, details the stories behind each one, and offers a humorous and fascinating insight into the cultural history of China. From paper tigers to praying mantis, to the music of nature and heavenly robes, these tales reveal aspects of Chinese thought and ancient customs. So, for those who delight history, and are eager to understand the origins of language as they learn it, the book *One Hundred Chinese Idioms* provides an excellent way of "killing two birds with one stone."

按 图 索 骥
àn   tú   suǒ   jì

A Winged Steed

The idiom *An Tu Suo Ji* originated with a father and son who became famous in ancient times, and still well known to Chinese today.

Bo Le, who lived during the Spring and Autumn Period (770-476 BC), was an expert at judging horses.

It is said that at just one glance, Bo Le could spot a "winged steed," (an outstanding animal that could run 300 miles a day) from a thousand galloping horses.

So today, his name is frequently used to praise persons who have a "good eye" at discovering talented young singers, dancers, athletes, artists, scientists or anyone who has an unusual gift in a specific field.

Bo Le had a son. Unlike his father, the son had no outstanding qualities at all and was known as a good-for-nothing.

However, like his father, the son is also remembered today by many Chinese people because of his involvement in the idiom *An Tu Suo Ji*, or "looking for a steed according to a picture".

As the best horse breeder of his time, Bo Le was not only respected by his peers but also by the duke of the State of Qin. One day, the duke said to him, "You are getting advanced in age, have you ever thought of passing down your exquisite skills to anyone?" Bo Le answered, "Yes, Your Excellency. But regrettably my only son is really a stupid boy and knows little about horses. So I will probably have to write down all my know-how and experiences if they are to benefit future generations of horse breeders."

With encouragement from the duke and after months of toil, Bo Le finished his book on horses. When the son saw it, he read a few chapters on how to determine which horses could be tamed into "winged steeds". According to the book, a potential "winged steed" should have a strong brow and deep-set eyes. There was also a picture in the book depicting this part of such a steed.

After copying the picture, the son decided to go out to find a "winged steed" so that he could become a master horse breeder like his father.

However, after wandering around for a whole day, he failed to find a single horse that fit the description and the picture.

On his way home, the son suddenly saw a big toad sitting on the roadside. He found the toad had a strong brow and deep-set eyes similar to the ones in the picture. He was overjoyed at his discovery and he ran into his father's room shouting, "Dad! Dad! I've just found a 'winged steed'!"

"Really? Where is it?" Bo Le asked suspiciously.

"Just in front of our house. Come on, Dad, let's go and see."

Going outside, the son pointed to the toad and said that the amphibian fit the description of a "winged steed" in the book, except for its legs, which did not look quite like those of a horse.

By letting out a long sigh, Bo Le said, "My son, you did very well. But the only problem is that the 'winged steed' you have found can only hop around, and you will never be able to ride it."

Today, people often cite the idiom *An Tu Suo Ji* to describe any single-minded dogmatist who brings back a toad when asked to find a "winged steed".

百 步 穿 杨

bǎi　bù　chuān yáng

Shooting a Willow Leaf

There must be hundreds of ways to evaluate a sharp-shooter. But for the Chinese, the sole qualification for an expert marksman is *Bai Bu Chuan Yang* or "to pierce a willow leaf with an arrow from the distance of 100 paces".

The expression is derived from a story about a legendary archer named Yang Youji.

Yang lived in the State of Chu during the Spring and Autumn Period (770-476 BC). He started to practice martial arts and archery when he was just a child. As he grew older, Yang became a top archer in his home district.

One day, Yang watched a group of young archers compete near his home.

First, they shot a target erected beneath a willow tree at a distance of about 50 paces. Most seemed to do quite well, so it was difficult to judge who was the best archer.

Yang suggested someone paint a willow leaf red and then the competitors shoot at the leaf from the distance of 100 paces.

One by one, the archers tried and failed to hit the red willow leaf which was quivering in the gentle breeze.

"Let me have a try," Yang finally said.

Taking the bow, he held his breath and concentrated on the crimson willow leaf. When he slowly released his grip, the arrow flew through the air with a powerful whoosh and pierced a hole in the leaf.

Loud applause burst from the onlookers.

However, one of the young archers dared Yang to shoot down more willow leaves to prove he was really a sharp-shooter. Yang agreed.

He collected a 100 arrows and then shot them one after another. All people present were awed to see that out of 100 shots, Yang had 100 bullseyes.

Since then, *Bai Bu Chuan Yang* has become a widely-quoted expression to describe an expert marksman regardless whether he uses an arrow, a stone, a knife, a gun or a rocket.

班 门 弄 斧
bān mén nòng fǔ

Master Carpenter

To explain the origin and meaning of the Chinese idiom *Ban Men Nong Fu*—or, to show one's proficiency with the axe before Lu Ban —we must first introduce you to two great names in the Chinese history.

One is Lu Ban, a legendary master carpenter, and the other is Li Bai, one of the greatest poets the Chinese nation has ever produced.

Lu Ban lived in the State of Chu around the time that the Spring and Autumn Period (770-476 BC) was replaced by the Warring

States Period (475-221 BC). As a carpenter, Lu had a pair of extremely dexterous hands.

To help his state battle its enemies, the carpenter invented various weapons, such as tactical push-hooks for fighting on boats and scaling-ladders for attacking walled towns. In addition, he created a number of carpenter's tool and helped build many famous bridges and palaces in the state.

Later, Lu was remembered by successive generations as the father of Chinese carpentry and the best carpenter in Chinese history.

Li Bai (AD 701-762) was a highly gifted poet during the Tang Dynasty (AD 618-907), the golden age of Chinese poetry. After his death, people built a beautiful tomb for him on the bank of the Caishi River.

Almost every day, throngs of his admirers visited the tomb. And more often than not, they scribbled one or two poems on the tombstone as if visiting it had given them some fleeting inspiration.

One day during the Ming Dynasty (1368-1644), a scholar called Mei Zhihuan also came to visit Li's tomb. When he found the tombstone was almost totally covered by poorly written poems, he decided to add one to the "anthology" to stop future visitors from writing any more.

Mei's poem reads to the effect, "A tomb near the Caishi River marks the everlasting fame of Li Bai; to and fro, every passer-by writes a poem on the tombstone just like a poor carpenter trying to show his proficiency with the axe before Lu Ban."

Although the scholar's poem did not stop people from continuing to write poems on Li Bai's tomb, his expression has since become a popular idiom in the Chinese language. Today, *Ban Men Nong Fu* is cited either to ridicule someone who displays his slight skill before an expert or to express one's modesty when demonstrating a skill in front of colleagues.

别 开 生 面
bié　　kāi　　shēng　miàn

Drawing New Faces

The Chinese idiom *Bie Kai Sheng Mian* is now widely used to describe someone who adopts a new style or breaks a new path

particularly in the creation of art or literature.

The original meaning of the expression, however, was to retouch an old painting to make it shine again.

Cao Ba was a legendary artist who lived during the Tang Dynasty (AD 618-907). Cao started to study Chinese calligraphy and painting when he was a just child. Later, he became known for his fabulous paintings of people and horses.

In AD 718, Emperor Xuanzong invited Cao to paint at the imperial court. Watching Cao at work, the emperor was so impressed that he declared Cao the designated painter to the court.

As a result, only a few of Cao's creations could be found outside the imperial court. Owners of his paintings were held in high regard.

Near the imperial court, there was a grandiose pavilion which was famous for its beautiful frescoes depicting the 24 heroes who helped establish the Tang Dynasty. After decades of exposure to the elements, the plaster had begun to peel and the colour started to fade.

One day, Emperor Xuanzong asked Cao to recreate the murals in the pavilion.

After spending days studying the old paintings and reading all the background material available about the 24 heroes, Cao undertook the royal assignment.

When his work was completed, the new paintings caused an enduring sensation. Some of the figures were so vivid that viewers felt they could almost step from the wall.

To show his royal appreciation, the emperor named the artist General Zouwuwei.

Several years later, Du Pu, a famous Chinese poet, wrote a poem praising Cao. One of the verses used the expression *Bie Kai Sheng Mian* to describe how the artist vividly recreated the faces of the heroes.

While Cao was immortalized, his later years were not entirely happy ones.

As an old man, he was expelled from the imperial court because he offended the emperor over a minor matter.

Despite his advanced age, Cao was forced to make his living by drawing portraits of passers-by in the street.

兵 不 厌 诈
bīng　bù　yàn　zhà

Nothing too Deceitful

There are many Chinese sayings about war and combat strategy. *Bing Bu Yan Zha* or "in war nothing is too deceitful" is but one of them.

This expression was first uttered by a general living in the Eastern

Han Dynasty (AD 25-220).

Under the rule of Emperor An, Qiang people in the northwest border areas organized a revolt and started to invade the inland provinces. Yu Xu, a general stationed in Wudu, was ordered to suppress the rebellion.

Learning that Yu was heading to today's Gansu Province with 3,000 soldiers, the rebels decided to ambush the royal troops in a valley. However, after receiving a secret report about the rebels' plan, the general ordered his troops to stop marching ahead and asked a number of local people to help spread the word that he was requesting the emperor send him more troops.

The rebels believed the story and cancelled their plans to ambush Yu.

Soon afterwards, the rebels withdrew from their positions and Yu and his troops quickly passed through the valley and headed to the heartland of Gansu.

While marching ahead at a speed of more than 50 kilometres a day, Yu ordered his men to leave behind more field stoves with each passing night to give the enemy the wrong impression that he was constantly getting reinforcements.

Since the number of rebel troops totalled nearly 10,000 men, more than triple the number of Yu's men, Yu first tried to avoid direct confrontation with the rebels and then selected a favourable location for a decisive battle.

He ordered his soldiers to first use weak bows to encourage the enemies to move closer. When they did, Yu's men switched to strong bows to kill more of the enemy.

Many of Yu's tactics were quite different from those used by earlier military strategists.

So, one of Yu's aides asked what his principle was in adopting appropriate tactics. The general responded: "In war, nothing is too deceitful."

博　士　买　驴
bó　　shì　　mǎi　　lǚ

A Donkey Receipt

Two interesting sayings in the Chinese language are often used to deride writing crammed with empty verbiage.

One likens such works to the bandages that once bound women's feet—both the writing and the bandages are said to be long and smelly.

The other is the idiom *Bo Shi Mai Lü*, or "a court academician buys a donkey". To understand the idiom, one must know the story behind it.

Yan Zhitui was a famous writer during the Northern Qi Dynasty (AD 550-577), who advocated a simple and to-the-point style of writing. He was appointed to several important posts at court when

he was young. Later, due to the then-turbulent political situation, he decided to retire to his hometown to concentrate on teaching the young people of the Yan family.

At that time, an abstruse and verbose writing style was the vogue. Young people in the Yan family were blindly following the trend. To persuade them to adopt a simple and straightforward style, Yan told them a story about a court academician.

One day, the court academician went to buy a donkey at a farmers' fair. After sealing a deal with a trader, the scholar asked for a receipt. The trader told him, "Sorry, sir, I can't write. Why don't you write the receipt for me since you are a learned man?" The scholar agreed.

The trader immediately bought paper and a brush for the academician. The scholar sat down on the roadside and began to write the voucher. He wrote on and on, and he soon attracted a group of curious onlookers.

The trader became impatient and asked the scholar, "What are you writing? Could you read out loud what you have already written down for me?"

"Yes, of course," the scholar answered.

Then, as if he were declaiming a poem, he read the three pages that he had just written. But after he finishing reading, the trader had not heard a single word about a donkey. So he asked again, "Sir, why don't you simply say that on this date, I sold a donkey to you and charged you a certain amount of money? What are the three pages of rubbish all about?" Hearing this conversation, the onlookers all burst out laughing.

After telling the story, Yan asked the young people, "Is there one among you who wishes to walk in the footsteps of the court academician?"

Today, even though it originated some 14 centuries ago, the idiom *Bo Shi Mai Lü* is often used by Chinese people to satirize pieces of writing in the style of that donkey receipt.

跛 鳖 千 里
bǒ biē qiān lǐ

A Lame Turtle's Conquest

In English, there is a fable about a race between a tortoise and a hare. The Chinese version pits a lame tortoise against six steeds.

The Chinese story has also inspired a popular idiom, *Bo Bie Qian Li*, or "a lame turtle goes a thousand miles," praising perseverance and unremitting struggle towards a set goal.

The story goes like this:

Many years ago, there were six steeds living in a mountainous region in central China. One day, the horses decided to leave their home to look for a better place to live.

But after walking into an expanse of woods with no obvious road ahead, the six could not decide where to go.

Suddenly, they heard a greeting—"Hello, and good morning" —uttered by a crippled tortoise inching his way along a winding path.

"Where are you going?" one of the horses asked.

"I've been told there's a paradise for animals in the south and I'm now on my way there," the reptile replied.

"Do you know where it is?" the horses asked.

"Not exactly," the tortoise said. "It's about one or two thousand miles away."

"Traveling at such a slow pace, do you think you can ever reach there?" one of the steeds asked.

"Yes, as long as I keep on going," the tortoise answered.

After the conversation, the tortoise continued his long march while the six steeds engaged in a heated discussion about how they could find a shortcut to the paradise.

The red horse suggested they go south. But the grey horse wanted to head west. The black horse said east seemed most promising. The remaining three argued over the best course of action to take.

The debate went on and on, in the woods where the six equines met the lame turtle.

Meanwhile, the turtle kept heading south.

After three years, it found the legendary paradise and settled down. But in paradise, the turtle did not find the six steeds it met in the woods.

Each morning it climbed to the top of a hill and looked to the north hoping to spot the horses. They never appeared.

Today, the expression *Bo Bie Qian Li* is used to encourage people in poor conditions to resolutely pursue their goals.

沧 海 桑 田
cāng　hǎi　sāng　tián

The Sea and Land

There are perhaps hundreds of ways to describe the constant changes in world events. The Chinese idiom *Cang Hai Sang Tian*, "the blue seas and the mulberry orchard", is an attempt at just this.

This expression comes from an ancient Chinese legend. The story says that in ancient times there was an immortal called Wang Fangping. One day, Wang decided to visit a man whose name was

Cai Jing.

Before the immortal's arrival, the Cai family first heard divine music drifting down from the heavens. Then they saw a group of musicians riding on the back of Chinese unicorns descending into their compound. A moment later, Wang and his entourage arrived.

Wearing a five-colour ribbon, Wang was seen sitting in a chariot drawn by five dragons. All his guards were big fellows carrying various kinds of flags.

When Wang set his feet on the ground all his entourage, including the musicians, vanished. Wang ordered an invisible servant to invite Ma Gu to join him for the dinner.

The Cai family guessed that Ma Gu must be another immortal and they were eager to discover what Ma would look like.

A few minutes later, they heard the invisible servant telling Wang that Ma Gu was inspecting Penglai, a legendary divine island lying in the East Sea and that she would come to join Wang as soon as she finished the inspection.

When Ma Gu came, Cai and his family was surprised to see that Ma was in her late teens and wearing a beautiful gown made of rare embroidered silk.

Wang greeted the girl and ordered the invisible servants to serve dinner. During the dinner, the girl told Wang that since she became an immortal, she had seen the vast East Sea turn into a huge mulberry orchard and then became sea again three times.

"During my last inspection tour, I found the sea had become shallow again. I suspect it will soon turn into a continent again. And I'm sure such changes will go on forever," said the divine girl.

After the dinner, the two immortals said good-bye to the Cai family and left in the same manner as they arrived.

Today, few Chinese remember this pedestrian legend, but most of them know the saying *Cang Hai Sang Tian* or "the blue sea and mulberry orchard" which derives from the immortal girl's comment on the changing East Sea. Philosophers believe that this is mainly because the expression can help people to understand the transiency of a man's life in comparison to the relatively eternal universe.

城 门 失 火

chéng mén shī huǒ

City Gate Fire

It happens quite often that someone is victimized for reasons which sound far-fetched or irrelevant. The Chinese idiom *Cheng Men Shi Huo* or "the city gate catches fire" is a good description of such a circumstance.

Actually, this saying is only the first part of an expression concerning the death of the fish in the moat surrounding the city gate.

Behind this popular Chinese saying is the following story:

Once upon a time, a city gate in the State of Song caught fire. Many people living in the neighbourhood rushed to the site carrying basins, pails and various kinds of vessels to help fight the fire.

However, they could not find any water nearby, except that of the moat. So they formed a long queue to bring the water from the moat to the site of the fire.

It took nearly half a day to bring the raging fire under control and by the time they did, the moat was completely dry.

It was then that the people realized that all the fish in the moat had died in the process. Some had been thrown into the fire and some had perished at the bottom of the moat.

Any others had been taken home by firefighters as a windfall.

This incident was described in an article by a scholar in the Northern Qi Dynasty, Du Bi, who coined the phrase, *Cheng Men Shi Huo, Yang Ji Chi Yu*, which means when "the city gate catches fire, the fish in the moat suffer," illustrating a situation where innocent bystanders can get into trouble, even if they are at a distance.

Nowadays, this expression is still widely quoted in both written and spoken Chinese, partly because of the vividness of the saying itself and partly due to the fact that "fish" still die in situations like a city gate catching fire.

重 蹈 覆 辙
chóng   dǎo   fù   zhé

Following the Track

Although many young pupils in China today are unlikely ever to drive an animal-drawn cart in their lives, they are still frequently advised by their teachers or parents to guard against *Chong Dao Fu Zhe* or "following the track of the overturned cart."

This idiom is based on a story about a group of eunuchs during the Eastern Han Dynasty (AD 25-220).

It was a unique political phenomenon in Chinese history that eunuchs in the imperial court often formed cliques to monopolize power and meddle in state affairs. At the same time, they tried all

means possible to turn the ruler into the so-called "puppet emperor".

During the Qin Dynasty (221-206 BC), Hu Hai, the son of the First Emperor of Qin, who built the Great Wall, was a typical "puppet emperor".

Hu was installed on the throne by a small number of eunuchs who forged the will of the First Emperor of Qin, and was forced to commit suicide three years later.

A similar situation appeared under the rule of Emperor Huan of the Eastern Han Dynasty.

In the court of Emperor Huan, the eunuchs were very powerful. They did not only bend the laws for individual interests, but also brutally suppressed any people who dared to criticize or oppose them.

In AD 166, the eunuchs framed a case against hundreds of officials and ordinary people, who were later all put into prison on charges of "establishing secret cliques and defaming the imperial court."

After learning about the case, Dou Wu, father of the then empress and an upright official, decided to file a protest to the throne.

In the document, Dou scathingly denounced the eunuchs' behaviour and warned the emperor if he failed to draw lessons from Hu Hai's experience, he might "follow the track of the overturned cart."

In addition, Dou presented his resignation to the emperor, vowing he would never serve in the same court with such "villains".

Under great pressure from both in and outside the court, Emperor Huan personally repealed the case and ordered the release of all those imprisoned by the eunuchs.

Today, the idiom *Chong Dao Fu Zhe* is often cited to advise people to draw lessons from the failures of others and avoid following the same road to ruin.

唇 亡 齿 寒
chún　wáng　chǐ　hán

Lips and Teeth

Chinese tend to describe close relations between two neighbouring countries as that of lips and teeth (*Chun Chi Xiang Yi*). This metaphor is actually derived from a popular idiom *Chun Wang Chi Han* (after losing the lips, your teeth will be exposed to the chill in the air), itself based on a bloody historical event.

During the Spring and Autumn Period (770-476 BC), Duke Jinxian of the State of Jin wanted to annex the neighbouring State

of Guo.

One of the Duke's officials said that the best way to capture the capital of Guo was to launch a surprise attack from the State of Yu, a close neighbour of Guo.

To kill two birds with one stone, the official suggested that the Duke ask the ruler of Yu to allow the troops of Jin to pass through his territory and then, after seizing the State of Guo, the Jin troops could easily wipe out the State of Yu on their way back. The Duke of Jin liked the plan and decided to follow the official's advice.

In order to persuade the ruler of Yu to allow the troops to pass, the Duke sent a special envoy to the State of Yu and offered the finest jade and his best horse as presents to the ruler.

A sharp-minded official in the court of Yu immediately became suspicious. He asked the ruler to decline the presents and reject the Duke's request. The official said that relations between the State of Guo and the State of Yu were just like those between lips and teeth. Once the lips were no longer in existence, the teeth would lose protection and be exposed to the chill in the air.

However, the ruler of Yu loved the jade and the horse so much that he turned a deaf ear to the warning and decided to allow the passage to the Jin troops.

After hearing of the ruler's decision, the sharp-minded official gave out a long sigh and fled the state with his family. Before his departure, he told his close friends that the State of Yu would crumble within the year.

The surprise attack launched by the Jin troops proved successful and the State of Guo was overrun in just a couple of days. On their way back home, the Jin troops captured the ruler of Yu and conquered his state as planned. In captivity, the ruler of Yu regretted that he did not listen to the warning of "*Chun Wang Chi Han.*"

But it was too late.

从 善 如 流
cóng　shàn　rú　liú

Following Good Advice

The best advice you can give anyone is to tell them to follow good advice.

And in the Chinese language, there are a number of expressions to this effect.

One of them is *Cong Shan Ru Liu* or "follow good advice as naturally as a river follows its course".

People first cited this idiom to describe Ruan Ping, a Jin State official during the Spring and Autumn Period (770-476 BC).

In the later years of that period, the States of Chu and Jin were two big powers among the warring states. And with its military might, Chu kept annexing nearby small states.

In 585 BC, the Chu troops began to invade the State of Zheng, which turned to Jin for help. Since the small state had good relations with Jin, the Jin ruler decided to send troops to fight the invaders. Minister Ruan Ping was appointed commander-in-chief.

But as they approached, the Chu troops withdrew from Zheng to avoid a direct confrontation.

Ruan was furious and decided to attack a small state which was under Chu's protection.

This time, the Chu troops came to help and set up a defence line in the small state.

Ruan now had to decide whether to take them on, and as he pondered, three of his top aides came to see him and persuade him to back off. They pointed out that this time the Chu troops were fully prepared for battle and it was unwise to confront the dashing spirit of the enemy.

However, most of his other aides said otherwise.

After listening carefully to their opinions, Ruan decided to take the safe option and left the small state.

Someone asked Ruan why he followed the advice of a minority of his aides and rejected the majority.

The minister answered: "Only the correct opinion represents the majority."

"Although only three of my aides were for withdrawal, theirs was good advice. Therefore, they are true representatives of the majority."

Two years later, Ruan found a favourable opportunity to attack the Chu troops and won several decisive battles.

Later, a famous historian called Ruan a man who was ready to follow good advice.

Today, the saying *Cong Shan Ru Liu* is often used to depict anyone who follows what is good naturally and happily.

得 陇 望 蜀

dé   lǒng   wàng   shǔ

Insatiable Desire

Avarice knows no bounds. This universal truth is often heard in English, for example in the sayings: "appetite comes with eating," "much will have more" and "one conquest breeds the appetite for another," all of which reflect the insatiability of man's desires.

In Chinese, there are also a series of expressions of the same ilk. Of them, the idiom *De Long Wang Shu* or "To cover Sichuan after capturing Gansu" is perhaps the most popular one.

Sichuan and Gansu are two neighbouring provinces in China. The former is located in the southwest and the latter in the northwest of the country. The idiom first appeared in a war decree issued by Emperor Guangwu during the early years of the Eastern Han Dynasty (AD 25-220).

In the year AD 32, Emperor Guangwu personally led a large army to attack Longxi (today's eastern Gansu), an area which was then ruled by an opposition force under the command of Wei Xiao.

The royal army surrounded two strategic towns there, but failed to capture them because the enemy was reinforced by troops from Sichuan, another opposition stronghold.

After several months of standoff, the emperor became impatient and decided that he would return to the capital but leave his general, Cen Peng, to continue to attack two towns in the region.

Before his departure, Emperor Guangwu issued a war decree calling on the royal troops to invade Sichuan after seizing the two towns. The emperor said in the document: "A man's desire is very hard to satisfy. Therefore, after capturing Gansu, one would wish to take Sichuan."

The two strategic towns proved to be tough nuts to crack. After several bloody battles, the royal troops had to retreat.

Four years later, the son of the opposition leader Wei Xiao surrendered to the imperial court. General Cen Peng seized this opportunity to conquer both Gansu and Sichuan. So, finally, Emperor Guangwu's desire of "covering Sichuan after capturing Gansu" was satisfied.

Today, the idiom *De Long Wang Shu* has a derogatory denotation and it is often quoted to describe people who are greedy and nurture insatiable ambition.

东 施 效 颦

dōng   shī   xiào   pín

Imitating Beauty

In Chinese history, there were a number of famous beauties. Many of them have survived thousands of years in forms such as poems, novels, dramas and idioms. *Dong Shi Xiao Pin* or "Dong Shi imitates eyebrows knitting" is but one example.

This expression is based on a story dating back to the late years of the Spring and Autumn Period (770-476 BC).

Xi Shi was an acclaimed beauty who was born and brought up in the State of Yue in eastern China. Throughout her life, Xi Shi had been involved not only in romantic anecdotes, but also in some intricate political plots. However, she was best known for her peer-

less beauty.

The story goes that before she was presented to the king of the State of Wu as one of his concubines, Xi Shi suffered from some sort of heart trouble. Therefore, she was often seen knitting her brows and walking across the village with a hand on her chest.

But, people found instead of eroding her striking beauty, the eyebrow knitting had bestowed a unique type of charm upon the young woman.

Dong Shi, an ugly woman living in the neighbourhood, had the same feeling. Having long been a hearty admirer of Xi Shi, Dong Shi decided to imitate her idol's eyebrows knitting and her way of walking. She thought this might help disguise some of her ugliness.

But the blind imitation only made Dong Shi uglier. And whenever Dong Shi was walking across the village with her eyebrows knitted and a hand on her chest, the rich people would shut their doors and the poor would turn away to avoid seeing the detestable contortion of her face.

The story concludes: "Alas, that woman mistook frowning for something invariably beautiful, and was unaware that it only adds beauty to a real beauty."

Since then, the expression "Dong Shi imitates eyebrows knitting" has gradually become a popular idiom.

Nowadays, the idiom *Dong Shi Xiao Pin* is often quoted to warn people that blind imitation may lead to ludicrous effect. And as long as this idiom still lives in the Chinese language, Dong Shi will remain to be the symbol of playing the ridiculous ape.

对 牛 弹 琴
duì　niú　tán　qín

Cattle Music

One interesting thing is that no matter how difficult two languages are, one can always find matching expressions.

For example, when English speakers say "to beat your head against a brick wall," "to cast pearls before swine" or "to eat gravy with a fork," the Chinese are very likely to quote the idiom *Dui Niu Tan Qin* or "to play the lute to the cattle".

This idiom derives from a story that originally means one should address the audience with languages familiar to them.

Mou Rong was a well-known scholar who lived in the late years of the Eastern Han Dynasty (AD 25-220). He had spent many years

studying the Buddhist Scritptures.

One day, the scholar gave a lecture on Buddhism to a group of Confucianists. During the lecture, Mou never used a single word from the Buddhist sutra. Instead, he repeatedly quoted paragraphs and expressions from the Confucian classics to explain the gist of Buddhism.

One audience member interrupted Mou and asked him why he never used a single Buddhist term in his lecture.

Mou then told the audience a story.

"A long, long time ago, there was an accomplished musician who once played the lute to a group of cattle. But, the cattle kept grazing around and did not show any reaction to the music.

"After carefully observing the expression of the cattle, the musician realized it was not that the animals did not hear the music but that they could not understand it.

"Then, the musician started to play the lute imitating the sounds of gads, mosquitoes and houseflies. Immediately, the cattle stopped grazing and listened intently to the music."

The scholar concluded the story by saying that for the same reason, he had used the Confucianist terms to explain the Buddhist canon to a group of Confucianists.

Today, the idiom *Dui Niu Tan Qin* is still frequently quoted in both spoken and written Chinese. But, it now only means that someone is playing to the wrong audience, preaching to deaf ears or reading Shakespeare to a group of illiterate loggerheads.

釜 底 抽 薪
fǔ　dǐ　chōu　xīn

Root Cause

A very common headache that most people will face at one time or another is how to find a fundamental solution to an awkward predicament or, in other words, how to remove the root cause of a problem. If you ask the Chinese, they will tell you that the best way to do this is to "take away the firewood from under the pot" or *Fu Di Chou Xin*. They have been using this tactic for more than 1,400 years.

Hou Jing was a good friend of Gao Huan, who was a high-ranking official in the court of the Northern Wei Dynasty (AD 386-534). After the dynasty split into two states, namely, the Eastern Wei and the Western Wei, in AD 534, Gao became the ruler of the Eastern Wei and gave his friend Hou 100,000 troops and asked him to govern Henan Province.

Hou respected Gao, but did not like his son, Gao Cheng. So, when Gao Huan died 14 years later and was succeeded by his son, Hou decided to rebel against the court. He first tried to seek support from the Western Wei, but failed because the Western Wei ruler was suspicious of Hou's motives since Hou had earned himself a reputation as a "treacherous general".

Under the continuous offensives launched by the troops of Gao Cheng, Hou left Henan and surrendered to the emperor of the Liang Dynasty (AD 502-557) in the south. After learning about this, Gao Cheng sent a note to the emperor requesting Hou's extradition.

In the note, Gao Cheng told the emperor that Hou was a troublemaker and asked him to get rid of Hou. "To stop the soup from boiling, you'd better take away the firewood from under the pot; and to remove weeds, you'd better destroy their roots," Gao added in the note.

However, the emperor rejected Gao's request because he was planning to take advantage of the "Hou Jing Rebellion" to conquer the states in the north and to unify China. Later, Hou betrayed the emperor and ruined his plans for China unification.

Today, whenever people believe that drastic measures must be taken to solve a thorny problem or to deal with a complicated situation, they will resort to the tactic of *Fu Di Chou Xin*.

覆 水 难 收
fù　　shuǐ　　nán　　shōu

Spilt Water

It is a pity, more often than not, that a wrong step cannot be retaken or changed for the better.

In such a case, English speakers are likely to recall the saying, "It's no use crying over split milk," while most Chinese will cite the idiom *Fu Shui Nan Shou* or "Spilt water cannot be retrieved".

Unlike other Chinese idioms, this popular four-character phrase has three different stories explaining its origin.

Of the three, the most widely accepted is about a divorce case

involving one of the most famous strategists in Chinese history, who acheived success very late in his career.

Jiang Taigong, who lived during the late 11th century BC, married a woman named Ma when he was a poor young scholar.

Jiang cared little about material things and devoted almost all his time and energy to studying history and millitary strategies and tactics.

After living in abject poverty with Jiang for several years, Ma got fed up with this "bookworm", who was not likely ever to become rich or famous. So she divorced him and departed.

Jiang's brilliant talents were not discovered until he met King Wen of the Western Zhou Dynasty (llth century-771 BC). By that time, Jiang was already in his eighties.

Despite his advanced age, Jiang helped the king and his successor, King Wu, unite the kingdom and overthrow the Shang Dynasty (16th century-llth century BC).

To cite him for his meritorious service, Jiang was first appointed prime minister and later made the Duke of Qi.

After learning about Jiang's success, his ex-wife came to see him and plead for a reunion. At this, Jiang took out a basin of water and threw it on the ground.

Jiang told his ex-wife: "Only if you can gather up the spilt water will I agree to remarry you."

But all the weeping and rueful woman could gather up was mud. Gnawing by deep regret and sorrow, the woman left Jiang and never came back again.

A lesson that one can learn from the story, or the Chinese idiom *Fu Shui Nan Shou*, is that in order to avoid the predicament of "crying over spilt milk" or "retrieving spilt water," one should either look before leaping or never look back at all.

高　山　流　水
gāo　shān　liú　shuǐ

Mountains and Rivers

It may sound bizarre if someone likens a good friend or wonderful music to "high mountains and flowing rivers" (*Gao Shan Liu Shui*), but in China, *Gao Shan Liu Shui* is a popular idiom that comes from a touching story about Yu Boya, a legendary *guqin* virtuoso (a seven-stringed plucked instrument similar to a zither) who lived during the Spring and Autumn Period (770-476 BC).

When he was young, Yu loved playing the *guqin* and later became

a student of Cheng Lian, the best *guqin* player of the time.

Under Cheng's tutoring, Yu made remarkable progress and after three years of practice he had almost mastered the instrument.

However, Yu felt that he still wasn't a real *guqin* virtuoso and could not use it to freely express his emotions.

One day, Cheng told his student: "I have taught you whatever I know, but I can see that you aren't quite satisfied. So, I'll recommend you to another teacher who can bring you to the perfection of *guqin* performance."

Next morning, Cheng took Yu to the top of a high mountain cliff bordering on the sea in the east. Cheng told Yu: "You wait here and your new teacher will arrive in a few minutes." Then Cheng went away leaving Yu alone on the top of the mountain.

Yu waited and waited, but no one appeared. Then, gradually, he became enthralled by the beautiful melodies created by the sound of the sea waves crashing on the rocks below and the song of the birds and whispering leaves in the nearby woods. When the sun began to set, it suddenly dawned upon Yu that the new teacher recommended by Cheng was none other than nature herself. Yu realized that only by learning from nature could he master the real virtuosity of the *guqin* and so found an inexhaustible source of inspiration and energy.

Yu finally reached the level of perfection he was seeking *guqin* and became the best *guqin* player of his time. But, because of the profundity of his musical works, Yu found few people could really understand them. Only his bosom friend, Zhong Ziqi, could actually appreciate his talents.

When Yu was playing a new tune one day, Zhong became very excited. He said: "It's wonderful, I can see lofty Mount Tai in front of me." Then, Yu played another tune and Zhong clapped his hands, saying: "Bravo! It's just as melodious as the flowing rivers."

Since then, people use "high mountains and flowing rivers" (*Gao Shan Liu Shui*) to describe a bosom friend like Zhong Ziqi or wonderful music such as that created by Yu Boya.

Later, when his friend Zhong died, Yu wept. He told others: "Now that my friend Zhong is gone, why should I play the *guqin* any more?" So he broke his beloved instrument and never touched another *guqin* for the rest of his life.

狗 尾 续 貂

gǒu　　wěi　　xù　　diāo

Dog's Tail

In English, there are many expressions based on dogs: "died like a dog," "in the doghouse," and "It's a dog's life." In Chinese, there is also a popular saying relating to this animal and it has to do with the "dog's tail".

The Chinese saying, *Gou Wei Xu Diao* or "substituting dog's tail for sable" grew out of a fierce and complex power struggle in the court of the Western Jin Dynasty (AD 265-316).

When Sima Yan became the first emperor of the Western Jin Dynasty, he granted titles and territories to a large number of nobles. This was because the new emperor believed such measures

would encourage these nobles to help consolidate his rule and pay hefty tribute to the imperial court.

But actually, the emperor's decision later led to widespread separatism and furious factional strife.

After Sima Yan died in AD 290, the power struggle in the court escalated out of control and in less than 10 years, the throne changed hands several times. Members and relatives of the royal family all seemed to be involved in some sort of dirty plotting or even cold-blooded murder in order to seize the power of the throne for themselves.

In AD 300, Sima Lun, who was then in control of the royal army, staged a successful coup and named himself the new ruler. Like the first emperor of the dynasty, Sima Lun granted titles to several thousands of his followers. As a result, the court soon ran out of its supply of the official seals needed for the certificates of appointment and the sable used to decorate the hats of royal officers.

In the face of this unexpected problem, the emperor decided to use white-painted wooden plates to replace the metal seals and dog's tails as a substitute for the sable. People immediately began to ridicule the makeshift measures of the imperial court by coining the phrase about "substituting sable with dog's tail".

Although the Western Jin Dynasty was ill-fated and brief compared to other dynasties in Chinese history, it did leave a legacy, since the saying about the "dog's tail" still lives on in the Chinese language today.

Now, the idiom *Gou Wei Xu Diao* is used most often to criticize those who create a sadly-lacking sequel to a time-honoured masterpiece.

邯 郸 学 步
hán   dān   xué   bù

Learning to Walk

When a youngster tried to copy the way people walked in a neighbouring state, he never expected that he would end up having to crawl all the way home, but he did. This is the story behind the commonly-cited Chinese expression *Han Dan Xue Bu*, meaning "learning the way they walk in Handan".

The legend has it that in ancient times, the people living in a place called Handan in the State of Zhao had a unique, beautiful way of walking. When he heard about this, a youngster from the State of

41

Yan decided to travel all the way to Handan to learn how to do it.

When he got there, the youngster spent several days in the streets observing the local folks and found their gaits to be extremely graceful. So he began to imitate their strides and the way they moved their legs and arms.

Despite his persistent efforts, though, he failed to get the hang of it.

He decided this must be caused by the fact that he had grown up initiating the way his parents walked and to effectively learn a new way he must start from the very beginning.

So starting the next day, he began to follow the steps of toddlers instead of grown-ups. Strolling down the street became a complicated piece of foot work for the youngster. Before taking a step, he had to stop to think of how to put his foot, how long his stride should be, how he should move his head, his body and arms.

The situation went from bad to worse as he continued his efforts for a few more weeks, and the youngster found that not only could he still not walk the way the Handan people did, but he also forgot his original way of walking.

When he finally gave up, he found he didn't know how to walk at all any more, so as a result, he ended up having to crawl all the way home.

Nowadays, the idiom *Han Dan Xue Bu* is often used in describing anyone who imitates others obsequiously, losing his or her own originality.

画 虎 类 犬
huà　　hǔ　　lèi　　quǎn

Tiger and Dog

In many Chinese sayings, the tiger represents the powerful, the monarch or the upper class, while dog is deemed ignoble or lower class. *Hua Hu Lei Quan* or "try to draw a tiger but end up with the likeness of a dog" is a good example here.

The phrase is derived from a letter written by Ma Yuan, a well-known elocutionary scholar who lived during the Eastern Han

Dynasty (AD 25-220).

Because of his learnedness and eloquence, Ma was often summonded by the imperial court to discuss state affairs in front of the emperor. Two of Ma's nephews, Ma Yan and Ma Dun, admired their uncle's achievements and decided to follow his example and become elocutionists of his stature.

However, instead of discussing serious questions, the two young men were often heard passing judgement upon other's behaviours and personality.

Learning this, Ma was fearful that his nephews were heading in a wrong direction while pursuing careers as elocutionists. So, he wrote them a letter, hoping to persuade them to avoid passing judgement on others.

In the letter Ma said he would like to see his nephews learning from Long Bogao, a modest, upright and tight-lipped scholar who was respected by his peers. But Ma warned the young men they could turn out to be good-for-nothings if they tried to imitate Du Jiliang, another scholar of that time.

Ma said although Du boasted a heroic spirit and loved to help others, his behaviour was difficult to copy. This was just like someone trying to draw a tiger but ending up with the likeness of a dog.

Since the letter was made public, it has been read by nearly all Chinese scholars as a classic essay and the phrase *Hua Hu Lei Quan* has become a popular idiom.

Today, the saying is frequently used to describe poor imitations, to persuade people not to reach for what is beyond their grasp, or to bite off more than they can chew.

画 龙 点 睛

huà　lóng　diǎn　jīng

Eyes of the Dragon

The literal translation of the Chinese idiom *Hua Long Dian Jing* is "to dot the eyeballs while painting a dragon". The saying is now widely quoted to refer to adding the crucial touch to a work of art that brings it to life or putting in the word or two that clinches the point.

The expression is based on a legend about a famous painter, Zhang Sengyao.

Zhang was once an officer serving in the court of Emperor Liang Wu. But he was best known for his outstanding artwork.

It was said that whenever the emperor missed his sons who were away on official duties, he would ask Zhang to visit him and paint portraits of them. The pictures were so vivid that when the ruler saw them, he felt he was actually seeing the boys in person.

There also was a story about Zhang painting an eagle on the wall of a big temple in what is now Zhenjiang city in Jiangsu Province. It was said that the life-like eagle scared all the small birds away. Some even abandoned their nests on the roof of the temple.

One day, Zhang was painting four dragons on the wall of the Anle Temple in Jinling (now the capital of Jiangsu Province). The scene drew a large crowd.

In less than half a day, the artist had finished the painting. But although the onlookers all loudly praised the fine work of art, they were puzzled to find that none of the four dragons had eyeballs.

"Why don't you add eyeballs to the dragons?" asked one onlooker.

The artist answered: "If I added eyeballs to the dragons, they might fly away into the sky."

Few were convinced by that explanation, and some of them challenged the artist to prove just how a dragon in a painting could fly.

To convince the crowd, the artist went ahead and added eyeballs to two dragons on the wall and suddenly, a thunderstorm began and the two dragons took off from the wall and soared off into the dark, cloudy sky.

When the storm abated and the crowd recovered from the shock, they found only two dragons left on the wall—the ones with no eyeballs.

画　蛇　添　足

huà　　shé　　tiān　　zú

A Foot or Two Too Far

Hua She Tian Zu or "draw a snake with feet added to it" is perhaps the Chinese saying which can best express the truth that to overreach the mark is just as bad as not reaching it.

The story about the popular Chinese expression dates back to the Warring States Period (475-221 BC).

One day, after holding a ceremony of offering sacrifices to his ancestors, a lord in the State of Chu decided to give a goblet of wine to his servants as a reward.

The wine was not enough for all the servants, but it could well quench the thirst of one drinker.

Therefore, one of the servants suggested they hold a contest of drawing a snake on the ground and whoever finished first would take the goblet of wine as the prize. The others agreed.

Then each contestant took a branch of a willow tree as a pen and started to draw the snake on the earth ground. One of them did it very fast and finished his drawing in less than 30 seconds.

He took up the goblet and was ready to drink the wine. But, when he found others were still drawing their snakes, he said to himself "Aha, I still have time to add some feet to my snake before I enjoy my wine."

So, holding the goblet in his left hand, he used his right hand to supply his snake with feet.

However, before he finished the feet, another servant completed drawing the snake and snapped the goblet from his hand.

"A snake never has feet. Why are you adding feet to it?" asked the second servant. And with that, he guzzled down the wine.

The servant who first finished drawing his snake was dumbfounded and failed to make a reply. He regretted that he had lost the wine because he tried to gild the lily by adding feet to a finished picture of a snake. But, it was too late.

These days, the idiom *Hua She Tian Zu* is frequently quoted to depict any act which ruins the effect by adding what is superfluous.

鸡 犬 升 天
jī　quǎn　shēng　tiān

Chickens and Dogs

Nepotism, or showing undue favour when promoting one's relatives and friends to advantageous positions, is perhaps a universal social phenomenon. And the Chinese idiom *Ji Quan Sheng Tian* or "chickens and dogs also ascending to heaven" must be one of the most vivid expressions describing this phenomenon.

The Chinese saying is derived from a story about Liu An living

in the Western Han Dynasty (206 BC-AD 24).

Liu was a devoted follower of Taoism who wished to live forever.

In order to obtain immortality pills, he gathered together a large number of Taoist alchemists.

One day, eight white-haired old men came to see Liu, claiming they were the best alchemists of the day.

At first, Liu did not believe them. But when the eight visitors instantly changed into young boys, the royal descendant was convinced of their powers.

Liu was awed by what he saw and treated the eight Taoists as distinguished guests. He asked them to make pills that would give him immortality.

A few weeks later, the eight alchemists produced the pills.

Liu decided to hold a grand ceremony celebrating their achievement. He announced he would take two longevity pills at the gala.

Just then, a messenger rushed in and reported that Liu's residence was being stormed by royal troops who were sent to arrest him on charges of treason.

Liu was panicked. But the eight alchemists persuaded him to take a pill and leave the hall immediately.

After swallowing just one tablet, Liu flew into the sky with the eight alchemists.

In the confusion, the remaining pills dropped to the ground and were eaten by chickens and dogs wandering through the area.

In a few minutes, people saw the chickens and dogs ascending to the heavens and finally vanishing into the sky.

This story spawned the popular saying called *Yi Ren De Dao, Ji Quan Sheng Tian*, "When a man attains the Tao (enlightenment and immortality), even his chickens and dogs ascend to heaven".

Here the chickens and dogs mean mere dependents of someone who has just been lifted to a higher position.

Later, the saying was shortened to a four-character idiom *Ji Quan Sheng Tian*, which now is often cited to describe anyone who promotes his relatives or friends to high positions simply because he has the clout and power.

狡 兔 三 窟

jiǎo　　tù　　sān　　kū

Wily Hare

Despite their different cultural backgrounds, Chinese and English idioms are often surprisingly similar.

For example, while English people say "a hare with only one hole is soon caught," the Chinese have the idiom *Jiao Tu San Ku*, or "a wily hare has three burrows".

Most Chinese idioms boast a very long history, and this one about a "wily hare" dates back more than 2,000 years.

During the Warring States Period (475-221 BC), Meng Changjun

was prime minister of the State of Qi, and he had more than 3,000 proteges. Among them was a very clever person called Feng Xuan.

One day, Meng asked his proteges, "Who is willing to help me collect the capital plus interest that I have loaned to the people living in the Xue area?" Feng, who had long failed to attract the prime minister's attention, eagerly answered, "I'm willing to go." Then Meng told Feng that instead of bringing back the money, he could use it to buy whatever he deemed useful for his patron.

After arriving at the Xue area, Feng called all the debtors together in an open place and then he burned all the loan contracts in their presence. He told the people that the prime minister had decided to forgive them all their debts because of the poor harvests they had suffered in the past few years.

Most people present were moved to tears by the prime minister's generosity and sympathy, and they cheered in unison, "Long live the prime minister!"

When Feng returned to the capital, the prime minister asked, "What have you bought for me?" Feng answered, "I found you had everything except popularity, so I have burned all the loan contracts and brought popularity back to you." The prime minister was not happy about what Feng had done, but it was too late to change things.

One year later, Meng was dismissed by the King of Qi. Soon, the 3,000 proteges left him, and only Feng remained loyal to the disgraced official. Feng persuade his patron to move to the Xue area and the latter agreed.

After learning that the former prime minister was to settle down in there, local people went out nearly ten miles to greet him. Meng was very much moved by the warm welcome, and he told Feng, "Only today have I begun to really understand the value of what you bought for me last year."

But Feng said: "A willy hare has three burrows and a crafty man should have more than one hideout. I will build two more 'burrows' for you."

Later, the clever young man got the king to reinstate Meng as his prime minister and entrust him with the task of building an ancestral shrine for the Qi rulers.

After the shrine was completed, Feng told Meng, "Prime Minister, you have three 'burrows' and you may now sit back and relax."

金　城　汤　池
jīn　chéng　tāng　chí

Impregnable City

For centuries, strategists around the world have been wracking their brains to create an impregnable defence system. The American "Star Wars" system is one of the most well-known modern high technology systems. The Star Wars theory though is really not much more than an updated version of an old idea—to be truly impregnable.

An ancient version of such a defence system is described in the

Chinese saying, *Jin Cheng Tang Chi*, meaning "a city surrounded by metal ramparts and a moat of boiling water". This imaginary fortress was to have been first mentioned by a politician about 20 centuries ago.

During the late years of the Qin Dynasty (221-206 BC), Wu Chen, a rebel army general, planned to conquer dozens of towns in northern China.

Despite some initial success, General Wu found himself facing a number of strongly fortified towns where the imperial armies had put up tough resistance against the advancing rebel troops.

One day, Kuai Tong, a politician close to the commander of one of the areas under beige, called on General Wu. Kuai asked the general: "Do you intend to seize all the towns in Hebei area?"

"Yes, I do," answered the general.

"At the moment, you could only take one town after another through fierce fighting. But I can teach you a way to grab all of them with just one stroke."

"How?" the general asked eagerly.

Then, Kuai told the general that his friend, the commander of Fanyang, was inclined to surrender to the rebels, but he was afraid that he would be killed like other Qin officers in fallen towns. So, Kuai suggested that the rebel general offer the Fanyang commander nice treatment if he surrendered. He said this would set a good example and encourage other Qin commanders to follow suit.

"Otherwise," the persuader said, "the Qin troops would turn all the towns in the Hebei area into fortresses fortified with metal ramparts and moats of boiling water."

Since then, the expression, *Jin Cheng Tang Chi* has become synonymous with a city believed to be impregnable.

The rebel general followed the politician's advice and later seized more than 30 towns in northern China without a single military offensive.

The teaching behind the imaginary impregnable city story, however, is that an invulnerable defence system never exists.

54

锦 囊 妙 计

jǐn　náng　miào　jì

A Bag of Schemes

When consulting someone about solutions to urgent problems, the Chinese tend to ask, "Do you have any *Jin Nang Miao Ji?*"—that is, "Do you have any brilliant schemes in the brocade bag?"

The *Jin Nang* here does not refer to any ordinary brocade bag one could buy in a silk shop or department store. It is a very particular one made about 17 centuries ago by Zhuge Liang, one of the greatest military strategists ever brought forth by China.

During the Three Kingdoms period (AD 220-280), Zhuge Liang was the army adviser of Liu Bei, ruler of the Kingdom of Shu Han, which had seized a strategically located town called Jingzhou from

the Kingdom of Wu. Sun Quan, the ruler of Wu, sent an envoy to Shu Han to ask Liu Bei to return the town, but the envoy came back with only an IOU.

Feeling insulted, Sun decided to trick the newly widowed Liu into coming to the Kingdom of Wu by offering Liu in marriage his young sister. Sun planned to hold Liu hostage to force the Kingdom of Shu Han to return the town.

After receiving the invitation, Liu immediately realized that the marriage offer could be a trap, so he hesitated to go. But Zhuge Liang came forward to congratulate the ruler. He told Liu, "Your Excellency, you do not have to worry. I will ask General Zhao Yun to escort you to the Kingdom of Wu, and I will give him a brocade bag with some instructions inside to cope with emergencies."

Following the instructions in the brocade bag, General Zhao after Liu's arrival in Wu first sent people out to spread the news of the proposed marriage everywhere around the kingdom. As the royal marriage had become the talk of the town, the ruler of Wu had no choice but to have his sister marry Liu.

But, the ruler of Wu was not ready to give up. Sun ordered his aides to use delectable wines, beautiful women and exotic local entertainment to keep Liu in his kingdom as long as possible.

Again, following instructions in the brocade bag, General Zhao sounded a false alarm to Liu by saying that troops from a third kingdom, Wei, were about to attack Jingzhou. So Liu decided to immediately return to his own kingdom, together with his bride.

When the ruler of Wu sent his men to stop Liu and his entourage from going home, General Zhao asked the bride to come out to deal with the situation. Naturally, no officers from the Kingdom of Wu dared to offend the bride since she was their ruler's sister. This was also a scheme outlined by Zhuge Liang in advance.

Finally, Liu Bei returned to his kingdom with a beautiful bride and without yielding the town of Jingzhou.

Today, *Jin Nang Miao Ji* has become an idiom that often comes to mind when looking for ways to deal with an emergency. After all, is there anyone who does not wish to have a brocade bag such as the one offered by Zhuge Liang?

近 水 楼 台
jìn　　shuǐ　　lóu　　tái

Waterfront Towers

The Chinese idiom *Jin Shui Lou Tai*, meaning "the waterfront towers," refers to the importance of being in a favoured position.

The full phrase, *Jin Shui Lou Tai Xian De Yue* or "the waterfront towers get the moonlight first," comes from a poem written by a bureaucrat several hundred years ago.

Fan Zhongyan was a famous politician and scholar in the North-

ern Song Dynasty (960-1126) who had held several very important positions in the imperial court.

Fan paid great attention to promotion of young and talented officials. So many young aides who had once worked under Fan were later assigned to satisfactory positions thanks to the politician's recommendation.

Su Ling, a local official, was not happy about his job as a county inspector in the Hangzhou area, but he could not find a better job because of his lack of connections or strong recommendations. Therefore Su was jealous of the other young bureaucrats who had been helped by Fan.

One day, when Su was sent to submit a report to Fan, the young official was pleased to have the chance to see Fan and decided to take advantage of this opportunity to talk to the senior politician about his desire for a new job. But Fan was away. Su had to leave the report on Fan's desk and return to his own office.

Later, he wrote to Fan to express his desire for a more satisfying job. Enclosed was a poem with the lines, "The waterfront towers get the moonlight first; the flowers facing the sun tend to blossom earlier in spring."

Fan liked the verses very much and also understood very well their real meaning and soon recommended the young official to a better position.

Today, the phrase *Jin Shui Lou Tai Xian De Yue* is frequently used in talking about someone who enjoys the benefits of being in a favourable position.

举 棋 不 定

jǔ　qí　bù　dìng

A Hesitant Move

This comes from an ordinary scene of a chess player holding a piece mid-air in his fingertips, hesitating over what move to make. In the Chinese language this scene has been moulded into a popular idiom, *Ju Qi Bu Ding* or "holding a piece and hesitating".

This phrase was first quoted by a politician more than 2,550 years ago.

During the Spring and Autumn Period (770-476 BC), Duke Xian of the State of Wei was an arrogant and imperious ruler, who was

hated by most of his aides. In 559 BC, Ning Huizi and Sun Wenzi, two of the most prominent officials in the court, staged a coup and forced the duke into exile.

Then, Ning and Sun monopolized the power in the court and installed a young puppet ruler. But, several years later, when lying on his deathbed, Ning had a second thought about the coup and asked his son, who had already been promoted to a high position in the court, to help reinstate Duke Xian.

After the death of Ning, the deposed duke sent an envoy to see his son. The envoy told the young Ning that the old duke promised to offer him the post of prime minister in the court after his reinstatement and let him take control of all state affairs.

When the word spread that the young Ning intended to call back Duke Xian, many colleagues came to advise him against doing so.

One official said that the many years of exile had failed to change the old duke at all and he remained an arrogant and imperious man. In addition, he probably would not forgive the Ning family because of the old Ning's participation in the coup that dethroned him.

"First, your father opposed the duke and now you favour reinstatement of the duke. This is like a chess player holding a piece and hesitating in making a move. You'd better forget about such a plan," he told the young Ning.

Unfortunately, the young Ning was not convinced. He wanted to carry out his father's last instruction and cling to the post of prime minister promised by the old duke. Therefore, he welcomed back Duke Xian after killing the young puppet ruler and the family of Sun, who joined Ning's father in the coup.

Just as predicted by his colleagues, the reinstatement of Duke Xian only led to the ruin of Ning's career and his family.

Today, few people remember the name of the wise, prophetical politician, but his quotation about a hesitating chess player survives. Many Chinese tend to quote the idiom *Ju Qi Bu Ding* to describe anyone who is in two minds.

刻　舟　求　劍
kè　zhōu　qiú　jiàn

A Lost Sword

Like English proverbs, many Chinese idioms and sayings are rather philosophical. The idiom *Ke Zhou Qiu Jian* or "finding a lost sword by marking the gunwale of a moving boat" is perhaps a good example here.

The story behind this saying is recorded in Master Lu's Spring and Autumn Annals written centuries ago.

The story says that once a man in the State of Chu was crossing

a river in a boat. Accidentally, his sword slipped out of the sheath and fell into the river. He reached into the water immediately trying to catch the sword, but he failed.

The man loved his sword very much so he decided to retrieve it at any cost. But how would he do it? With sudden inspiration, he fished a small knife out of his pocket and made a mark on the side of the boat where he had dropped his sword.

When he found other passengers on the boat all watching him with puzzled expressions, he explained: "I've made a mark here because this is where my sword slipped into the water. Then later on I can retrieve it by looking at the location of the mark."

By and by, the boat went on and finally it reached its destination and stopped. The man jumped quickly into the river from the marked side of the boat to recover his lost sword. Of course, this proved to be a futile attempt, because the man had failed to realize that while the boat was moving, the lost sword was not.

The philosophy expressed in the saying *Ke Zhou Qiu Jian* is still quite significant today to the Chinese people, even though it is rarely brought up in conversations, speeches or articles. Almost every primary school pupil in China is required to recite it, in order to make sure they have learned to avoid making decisions without taking into consideration changes in circumstance.

困 兽 犹 斗

kùn　shòu　yóu　dòu

Like a Cornered Animal

A story told more than 2,500 years ago brought forth a Chinese expression, still quite popular today.

Kun Shou You Dou or "a cornered beast will fight" was first uttered by the then prime minister of the State of Qin in persuading the king to refrain from executing a general who had just suffered

a shameful defeat in the battlefield.

The State of Qin was a big power among the warring states at that time. In 579 BC, General Xun Linfu was ordered by the Qin ruler to rush to the rescue of a small neighbouring state which was attacked by troops from the State of Chu, another power at the time.

However, when General Xun and his troops arrived at the border of the neighbouring state, they were told that it had already surrendered.

Xun intended to launch an offensive against the Chu troops anyway, but his plan was opposed by some of his assistants.

Meanwhile, the Chu troops took advantages of the shilly-shallying by the Qin army and staged a surprise attack.

So General Xun and his army suffered a total defeat and returned to the State of Qin crestfallen.

The Qin ruler was angered by the bad news and ordered General Xun executed.

But before the order was carried out, the Qin prime minister came forward and told the king the following story:

He said the same thing had happened nearly 30 years ago, but then it was the Qin army that was victorious and the Chu ruler who was upset.

This battle took place in the State of Chu and the Chu general was defeated by the Qin troops. But instead of celebrating its triumph, the then ruler of the Qin worried because he thought the defeated general would be an even more frightening adversary now that the general was like a cornered beast.

But the Chu general was executed for his defeat. And when the Qin ruler found out he was overjoyed at what he felt was now a double defeat, for his enemy, the State of Chu.

After listening to the story, the king revoked his execution order.

Today, the saying *Kun Shou You Dou* is widely cited to mean that people at bay will put up a desperate fight.

滥 竽 充 数
làn　　yú　　chōng　shù

Phony Player

Some Chinese idioms can be used in both flattering and derogatory ways. *Lan Yu Chong Shu* is an example.

If someone uses this idiom to describe himself, it is a self-depreciatory expression that means, "I'm not good enough and not quite qualified, although I'm in this post".

However, when it is used to define others, it means "to pass oneself off as one of the players in an ensemble" or "being there just to make up a number".

The idiom was first used more than 2,000 years ago to describe the behaviour of a certain Nanguo living in the state of Qi. It was during the Warring States Period (475-221 BC).

The king of Qi loved to listen to *Yu*, ancient wind instruments, played in unison. He always employed more than 300 *Yu* players to perform at his court and offered them liberal pay and benefits.

Nanguo knew little about the instrument, but he envied the *Yu* players and wished to earn as much as they did. So he went to the court and told the king of Qi that he was an excellent *Yu* player and wanted to join the imperial ensemble.

The king was very happy that he could recruit a master *Yu* player. He asked Nanguo to play with the ensemble beginning the next day and offered the phony *Yu* player excellent pay.

Though he did not know how to play the *Yu*, during each performance Nanguo imitated the finger movements of other players and pretended to be playing very enthusiastically. The king of Qi appreciated Nanguo's "performaces" very much and never found out that he was a phony.

Later, the king died and was succeeded by his son, who was also a lover of the *Yu*. But the new ruler liked to listen to *Yu* playing in solo performaces. So he asked players in the imperial ensemble to perform one by one.

Before it was his turn, Nanguo left the court and ran away to hide in a remote area.

Today, *Lan Yu Chong Shu* can also be used to describe substandard goods that are mixed with quality ones just to make up a round number.

老 马 识 途
lǎo　mǎ　shí　tú

Horse Sense

Horses have been very helpful friends to man for aeons. They have provided not only valuable services, but passion and delight, as well. They also have played important parts in a number of expressions in many languages.

The popular Chinese saying, *Lao Ma Shi Tu* or "an old horse knows the way" seems to only refer to something of the natural character of the animal. But the story behind this expression tells how one old horse actually saved the lives of thousands of soldiers.

In 663 BC, Duke Huan of the State of Qi led a large army to invade the Guzhu Kingdom. Among the aides accompanying him was Guan Zhong, a sharp-witted and resourceful man.

The offensive was successful, but it took much time, because of the long distances involved and the complex, local geography. So, when the Qi troops finally were able to withdraw triumphantly, it had already become winter.

The biting cold of the wind had deprived the fields and mountains of their vegetation and, thus, the surrounding scenery was quite changed. Very soon, the entire Qi army found itself lost in a deep valley.

Half a dozen teams of scouts were sent out to find ways home, but all failed to fulfill their mission.

After a few days passed, the duke became impatient and worried

and so he summoned his advisers to find a solution. The heated discussion led nowhere. Finally, Guan stood up and said: "Someone told me once that old horses always know their way home. Why not find an old horse that had been serving the army since the very beginning and let it play the role of our guide?"

They found just such a horse, who miraculously, through the winding, bumpy paths, led the anxious troops out.

The story was the genesis of the popular Chinese idiom, *Lao Ma Shi Tu*, which today, is often cited to describe people who are experienced, who know the ropes and have the knowledge of a veteran.

老 生 常 谈

lǎo shēng cháng tán

A Mere Platitude

People often turn a deaf ear to a repeatedly-told story. The same is true with age-old idioms.

People tend to regard the sayings as platitudes. Chinese people call such banalities "Sunday school truth"—*Lao Sheng Chang Tan*—or the "commonplace talk of an old scholar".

The "old scholar" was none other than Guan Lu, a gifted pundit

who lived in the State of Wei during the Three Kingdoms period (AD 220-280).

Guan began to study astronomy when he was a child. He loved to draw the sun, the moon and other planets on the ground while other children were playing in the dirt.

When he was 15, Guan became a scholar. Soon thereafter, he was invited to a local magistrate's home to discuss classical literature and astronomy with more than 100 philosophers.

The academicians tried, and failed, to baffle the young man with difficult questions.

Guan became known throughout the State of Wei as a prodigy.

Later, two ministers in the imperial court asked the young scholar to tell their fortunes and career paths because they both had bad dreams the previous night.

Guan had learned the two officials were despised by their colleagues and subordinates because of their greed and viciousness. So, he told them their dreams indicated their future was very gloomy and they would soon encounter problems.

One minister became very worried, but the other tried to console him by saying "Don't take it too seriously. It's commonplace talk of a scholar."

However, several months later, both ministers were executed for their involvement in an aborted coup.

Guan subsequently told his friends that this was a typical example of how people ignored the truth expressed by a commonplace notion.

乐 不 思 蜀
lè   bù   sī   shǔ

Forgetting One's Home

People tend to become homesick when they move to new places.

But, sometimes, when they're having a very good time, they care less about home.

The Chinese idiom *Le Bu Si Shu* or "being so happy as to forget the home country" is often cited to describe such a feeling.

The phrase was first used by Liu Chan, the last ruler of the Kingdom of Shu, in the late years of the Three Kingdoms period (AD 220-280).

In AD 263, when the troops of the Kingdom of Wei seized a town near the capital of the Kingdom of Shu, Liu decided to surrender to the invaders.

Later, he was taken to Luoyang, the Wei capital, where he was offered a house and some servants because of his submission.

One day, Liu and his former aides went to visit the Wei prime minister to express his appreciation of the lenient treatment meted out to him by the Wei regime.

The Wei prime minister threw a dinner party for Liu. At the party, the prime minister ordered some artists to perform both Wei and Shu songs and dances. The performances made Liu's aides very homesick, and only Liu looked happy and seemed to be enjoying himself.

So, the Wei prime minister asked Liu: "Don't you miss your homeland of Shu?"

The former Shu ruler said: "No. I'm very happy here, so I do not miss Shu at all."

Other people at the party were surprised by his answer and looked upon him as a traitor.

In the Romance of the Three Kingdoms, there is a poem describing Liu as a "poor ruler who enjoyed his life abroad and forgot his own country".

Probably because of this, today the saying *Le Bu Si Shu* still has a derogatory connotation and often means someone who indulges in pleasure and forgets his home and duty.

梁 上 君 子

liáng　shàng　jūn　zī

Gentleman on the Beam

Liang Shang Jun Zi means a "gentleman perching on the beam," a euphemism for "thief". This idiom has come from a story about Chen Shi, an elderly official who lived in Eastern Han Dynasty (AD 25-220).

Chen was an upright man highly respected by his peers and subordinates. He was also very strict on family education for his children.

One night, when he was just about to go to bed, Chen heard a faint strange sound overhead. But out of the corner of his eye, he saw a thief perching on the beam. How to deal with the situation? Chen decided to take advantage of this opportunity to give his children a lecture on morality and traditional values. Therefore, he called in his sons and grand children.

The young people were all wondering what the old man was up to by gathering them in his bedroom at midnight. With a serious expression on his face, Chen told his offsprings: "People have to discipline themselves. Bad chaps are not born bad, but they have picked some bad habits, just like the gentleman now perching on the beam."

The thief was startled by Chen's remarks. He jumped down from the beam and kneeled in front of the old man, asking for pardon. Chen told the thief to mend his ways and turn over a new leaf in his life. Then he let the thief go.

Since then, the phrase "a gentleman perching on the beam" has been widely used by Chinese people as a euphemistical way of naming a thief.

两　袖　清　风
liǎng　xiù　qīng　fēng

Clean Hands

Before the advent of the modern age, Chinese people, particularly officials, scholars and women, used to wear gowns and dresses with very long sleeves. So among the thousands of Chinese sayings, there are quite a few that refer to the tradition. *Liang Xiu Qing Feng* or "with two sleeves of cool breeze" is one of them.

The expression was coined by Yu Qian (1398-1457), an upright and honest official of the Ming Dynasty.

Yu was born in Qiantang, today's Hangzhou, capital of Zhejiang Province, and he entered officialdom at what was considered the tender age of 24.

He quickly gained a reputation of being an official who had great compassion for the ordinary people. In addition, Yu won the distinction as a stalwart advocate of uncorrupt government.

He was appointed governor of several provinces before he was designated to a post in the imperial court.

On the eve of his departure, one of his aides came to bid him good-bye and advised him to bring with him some local specialities.

The aide said: "You will need them. You are new in the court and you will have to grease the palms of some influential bureaucrats if you want to introduce yourself to your colleagues and superiors in the court."

Hearing the aide's advice, Yu let out a long sigh, and said, "I don't have anything. So when I take office in the court, I can only bring the cool breeze in my sleeves with me."

During the ensuing years, Yu experienced many ups and downs in his career. He was eventually persecuted and put to death by corrupt eunuchs in the imperial court.

After his death, people could hardly find any valuable articles in his house even though he had been a high-ranking official for decades.

Nowadays, the expression *Liang Xiu Qing Feng* is frequently used to describe a penniless person or an official who has kept clean hands.

鹿 死 谁 手
lù sǐ shuí shǒu

Who Will Take the Deer?

"Our national football team will meet the South Korean ll in the final of the Asian Football Cup in Bangkok tomorrow evening."

"But right now it is still very hard to predict *Lu Si Shui Shou*," said a television sports commentator.

The Chinese idiom, *Lu Si Shui Shou*—or "at whose hand will the deer die?"—has become a favourite sports term, indicating that it is difficult to tell which team will emerge victorious.

This popular idiom can be used to describe the unpredictability of the result in any kind of competition, including war, salesmanship and even singing.

Just as in the countryside, whoever kills a deer takes home the spoils, the word "deer" in the idiom can mean power, prize, supremacy, victory, profit or any other winnings.

This idiom comes from a phrase first used by Shi Le (AD 274-333), ruler of the Later Zhao Dynasty. Born into a poor family of the Jie nationality, Shi was sold as a slave in northern China when he was young. Later, however, he became a general under the Emperor Liu Yuan of the Early Zhao Dynasty. However, in AD 329, Shi rebelled against and finally overthrew the rule of the Early Zhao. The general then became the ruler of the Later Zhao Dynasty.

Shi had little education. But he loved to have close aides read books aloud to him, particularly history books. As a result, he knew of many famed figures in Chinese history.

One day in the spring of 332, a group of envoys from other states came to pay respects to the ruler of the Later Zhao Dynasty and to express their states' desire for closer relations. Shi was very happy about this, so he ordered a grand banquet to entertain the envoys.

During the dinner party, Shi asked Xu Guang, a high-ranking official in his court, if he could compare his emperor with others in Chinese history in terms of merit and virtues. In order to please the ruler in the presence of foreign guests, Xu said: "Your Majesty, your merits and accomplishments are even greater than that of Liu Bang (the first emperor of the Western Han Dynasty 206BC-AD24). I can't think of any other emperors after Liu in Chinese history who can match your majesty."

"You're flattering me, Minister Xu," Shi said laughingly, "If I had ever had the chance to meet Liu Bang, I would have kowtowed to him and served him in his court like many other well known generals at that time."

"However, if I had met Liu Xiu (the first emperor of the Eastern Han Dynasty AD 25-220), we probably would have fought for the throne. It could have been very hard to say *Lu Si Shui Shou*."

洛 阳 纸 贵
luò　　yáng　　zhǐ　　guì

Paper Price Soars

There must be more than 100 ways to praise an exceptionally good piece of writing. Editors may give it prominent display in newspapers or magazines, with an eye-catching headline; critics may rack their brains for the most flattering words in the language; and

publishers may promote it to the top of the bestseller list.

In China, however, people usually hail such a work by citing a popular idiom, *Luo Yang Zhi Gui*, or "the price of paper soars in Luoyang".

This idiom was first used to salute a piece entitled "San Du Fu," by Zuo Si, who lived during the Western Jin Dynasty (AD 265-316). Zuo was a stammerer and ugly. But he wrote beautiful prose and was particularly good at writing Fu, a kind of descriptive prose interspersed with verse that was favoured by ancient Chinese writers.

Once, he spent an entire year writing an article called "Qi Du Fu" about the Capital of the State of Qi. This article won Zuo a reputation as an excellent writer.

Encouraged by success, Zuo decided to write a longer work entitled "San Du Fu" to describe the history, scenes, culture, people and customs of the capitals of the Three Kingdoms of Wei, Shu Han and Wu (AD 220-280).

To make it a literary gem, the writer spent a lot of time and effort on research. He even got a job as a librarian in Luoyang, the capital of Western Jin, so that he would have access to rare historical data and literature.

Zuo worked meticulously on every sentence and every paragraph of his prose. And he did not finish it until a decade later.

It was really a beautiful work, and it created a stir in writers' circles. Lu Ji, a famous writer of that time, used to look down on Zuo, but after reading his "San Du Fu," he thumped on his table and shouted out, "Bravo!" Other famed writers vied with one another for the honour of writing the preface for the piece.

Soon, it became so popular that almost all officials and rich families in the capital sent people to queue at paper shops to buy paper to copy it. Because the supply was running short, it was said, the shopkeepers raised prices several times.

Luo Yang Zhi Gui is undoubtedly a nice addition to terminology for praising good writing. But today it may also serve as a valuable hint to the paper-making firms: Want to make a bigger profit? Employ top-notch writers!

满 城 风 雨

măn   chéng   fēng   yŭ

A Town in a Rainy Day

Man Cheng Feng Yu (winds and rains sweeping across the town) is an idiom frequently used by Chinese to describe a situation in which sensational news suddenly becomes the talk of the town.

Comparing a town drenched with rain to a town where all the people are talking about the same subject—on street corners, in teahouses, offices, schools, kitchens and at the dinner (or mahjong)

table—is, one must admit, a nice analogy.

This saying was originally borrowed from a line of verse written by a highly gifted poet, Pan Dalin, during the Song Dynasty (960-1279). His poem was about an autumn scene in a small Chinese town.

Despite his great talent, Pan did not pursue fame or wealth. He lived in poverty throughout his life, though his poems won him an admirable position in Chinese literature.

One day, Pan's wife asked him, "What's the use of you writing poems day and night? You are not selling them and we can't turn the paper into food or clothes to feed our children and keep them warm."

Pan answered, "You know that in ancient times there were famous poets who refused to sell their poems for a few dou (decaliters) of grain. So why should you push me to sell my poems for fuel, food and clothes?"

It was late September. Outside Pan's window, chilly winds and rain were stripping the trees of their yellow leaves. Looking at the scene, the poet got a fleeting inspiration and quickly wrote down a line of verse: *Man Cheng Feng Yu Jin Chong Yang* or "As the Double Ninth Festival (9th day of the 9th lunar month) approaches, winds and rain are sweeping across the town."

Just then, someone knocked at the door. Pan's wife answered and came back to tell her husband that several bailiffs had come to collect rent and taxes. Pan had to come out to talk to the visitors and ask for further postponement of the payment. When he sat down again at his dilapidated desk, the poet could not continue to write the poem as words such as "rent," "taxes," "fuel," "food" and "clothes" kept swirling in his mind.

That night, a good friend came to visit Pan and asked him for a new poem. Pan gave him the only line of verse he had written that day.

People who read this line of verse all liked it very much, and it soon became a widely cited rhyme for describing autumn scenes.

Later, however, part of the line, *Man Cheng Feng Yu*, was turned into a popular Chinese idiom for describing a place flooded by talk about sensational news.

毛 遂 自 荐
máo　suì　zì　jiàn

Self-recommendation

In China, modesty has been deemed a virtue for thousands of years. Sometimes Chinese modesty even seems hypocritical: A veteran master of martial arts claims he is at the beginning of his career; or a Chinese host apologizes to his guests, over a table of ten dishes, for not having enough food to feed them.

In a country where people are reluctant to admit their abilities, only a few dare to volunteer their services for fear of seeming big-headed. So Mao Sui, who recommended himself to be an adviser to a local prince in 258 BC, is famous for his courage. His name is still remembered today not only in history textbooks, but also in the

popular idiom *Mao Sui Zi Jian* or "to offer one's service as Mao Sui did".

His story dates back to the Warring States Period (475-221 BC). When the State of Qin laid siege to the capital of the State of Zhao, Prince Pingyuan of Zhao was sent to seek help from the State of Chu.

The prince wanted to choose 20 guest advisers to go with him. But after calling 19 names, he could not find a twentieth person worthy of going.

Then, Mao Sui, one of the prince's several hangers-on, came forward and recommended himself for last vacancy.

The prince asked: "How long have you been with me?"

"Three years," he said.

"A capable person is like an awl," said the prince. "Once you put it into the cloth bag, its tip will immediately come out of it. So why haven't I heard of your name in these three years?"

"Because until today, I have never been put into the cloth bag like an awl," Mao said.

Other advisers laughed at Mao behind his back. But the prince decided to include Mao in his entourage.

His decision was wise. When the negotiations between the prince and the King of Chu came to a deadlock, Mao used a long sword and sharp words to convince the king to form a military alliance with the State of Zhao.

When he returned home, Mao became a hero and was treated by the prince as a guest of honour for many, many years.

Today, the idiom *Mao Sui Zi Jian* has become a somewhat complimentary expression in the Chinese language. People tend to cite the idiom to describe anyone who offers himself for a position or volunteers his services.

门 庭 若 市
mén   tíng   ruò   shì

Crowded Courtyard

Men Ting Ruo Shi or "The courtyard is as crowded as a market-place" is a Chinese idiom now often quoted to describe a much visited house, store or site.

This saying first appeared in a story about a self-critical prime minister in the court of the State of Qi during the Warring States Period (475-221 BC).

Prime Minister Zou Ji always wanted to know whether he was as handsome as his friend Xu Gong, who was reputed to be good-

looking. Therefore one day he asked his wife the question. His wife immediately said: "Yes. And in my eyes you are more handsome than Xu Gong."

Then, Zou asked his concubine the same question. The woman said: "Of course you are as handsome as Xu Gong."

Next day, a friend came to visit Zou. The Prime Minister asked the friend to pass his judgement on the same question. The friend said: "I don't think Xu Gong is as stately as you are."

However, Zou was still not convinced. So, a few days later, he invited Xu Gong to a dinner. After looking closely at his friend, the prime minister decided he was not as good-looking as Xu Gong.

Next morning, Zou went to see King Wei of the State of Qi and told him the story. Zou said: "Last night, I could not sleep and tried very hard to figure out why my wife, concubine and friend all lied to me. Now, I have come to the conclusion that this is because my wife flatters me, my concubine fears me and my friend wants to ask me a favour.

"From this I have also realized that Your Highness as the king of a large state like Qi must be more fooled by honeyed words than I for no one around you who does not flatter or fear you and does not intend to ask you favours."

The king agreed. Therefore, he decided to award anyone who would criticize him and his court.

During the first few days after the promulgation of the decree, hundreds of people went to the court to offer their criticism and the courtyard was as crowded as a marketplace.

The king awarded those people as he promised and carefully listened to their opinions. Also, the ruler constantly revised his policies by taking into consideration the wise ideas he had collected through the opinion soliciting campaign.

A few months later, the crowd in the courtyard began to thin out and a year later, almost no one came to make any criticism.

As the State of Qi became stronger with each passing day, the neighbouring states all sent their envoys to the court of the State of Qi to pay tribute to the king.

Historians say that the idiom *Men Ting Ruo Shi* represents an illustrating example of "conquest through peaceful means starting in the courtyard".

模 棱 两 可
mó　léng　liǎng　kě

To Please Both Sides

According to a maxim that originated in feudal China, anyone who wished to thrive in officialdom has to adopt an attitude called *Mo Leng Liang Ke* or "putting a hand on the edge of an object to grasp both sides of it".

Mo Leng Liang Ke, still a popular Chinese idiom, is an equivalent of the English saying, "To run with the hare and hunt with the hounds"—that is, to try to please both sides to a disagreement.

The idiom originated with a slick and sly minister in the court of the Empress Wu Zetian (AD 624-705). According to historical records, the Empress Wu was a very cruel ruler who persecuted hundreds of court officials whom she suspected of rebelling against her rule. Therefore, few officials, except for Minister Su Weidao, were able to stay in office for long.

In fact, Minister Su himself was demoted and even sentenced to prison by the Empress Wu for allegedly allying himself with some disgraced officials in the court. But, time and again, the minister was reinstated simply because he had never really chosen and become loyal to one side or the other.

One day, soon after Su was appointed prime minister by the empress, a young man came to ask him his secret of success. Recalling the ups and downs of his career, a thought flitted across the prime minister's mind. Putting his hand on the edge of the back of a chair, Su told the young man: "My son, in officialdom, you should never make a clear-cut decision. Like putting your hand on the edge of an object, you should try to grasp both sides of it. Otherwise, you may be punished for being loyal to just one side."

Soon, Su was nicknamed "Prime Minister Mo Leng" or "prime minister who feels the edge". But Su's philosophy failed to avert his ill fate. After the empress died in 705, Su was again demoted and appointed to an office in a remote county in Northwest China. He was never recalled to the capital.

Today the idiom *Mo Leng Liang Ke* is often used to describe anyone who adpots an equivocal attitude or any formulation that is ambiguous.

鸟 尽 弓 藏

niǎo jìn gōng cáng

When Birds Are Gone

Niao Jin Gong Cang or "to put away the bow after the birds are gone" is a Chinese expression referring to the practice of kicking out the assistants when their services are no longer needed. Fan Li, a well-known official during the Spring and Autumn Period (770-476 BC), was maybe the first person in Chinese history to truly understand the meaning—and importance—of this saying.

During the war between the State of Wu and the State of Yue in

eastern China, the King of Yue had two top officials, Fan Li and Wen Zhong. Soon after the State of Wu was conquered, Fan Li suddenly disappeared. At first, the King of Yue was worried that Fan might be trying to set up a sphere of influence of his own and rebel against the court. But later, after Fan's shoes and clothes were found along with a note on the bank of the Taihu Lake, the ruler thought otherwise. In that note, Fan said that since the ruler of the State of Wu committed suicide, there were only two persons who might cause problems to the King of Yue: One was Xi Shi, a famed beauty who was once sent to the State of Wu as a gift to soften the will of the now-dead Wu ruler, and the other was Fan himself. Xi Shi, because she might distract the King from state affairs and Fan, because he has too much clout in the court and could become a threat to the king's rule.

The note concluded by saying, "Now, I have helped Your Excellency get rid of both of them."

The king assumed from the note that Fan had killed the beauty and drowned himself in the lake. A few months later, though, Fan was heard from again. Wen Zhong, the king's other top aide, received a letter advising Wen to quit his post and leave the court as soon as possible.

"After the birds are gone, the bows will be cast aside, and after the hares are killed, the hunting dogs will be cooked," Fan wrote. "The King of Yue is not likely to share good days with his veteran aides."

Although Wen was relieved that his former colleague was still alive, he did not take Fan's advice seriously. It wasn't too long until the king began to think that with Fan's disappearance Wen was the only person who had too much power in the court and therefore, the king eventually brought pressure to bear and Wen ended up killing himself.

Fan owed his life to his deep understanding of the Chinese idiom *Niao Jin Gong Cang*. Legend has it that the wise official changed his name and lived the rest of his life with the famed beauty Xi Shi in virtual seclusion.

抛　砖　引　玉
pāo　zhuān　yǐn　yù

Brick and Jade

An illustration of the cleverness of the human mind can be found when a valuable trophy is netted at the expense of providing something cheap in advance. To an English-speaker, that means to use a minnow to catch a whale. But to Chinese people, that is expressed in the old saying, *Pao Zhuan Yin Yu* or "casting a brick to attract jade."

There are two or three different stories behind the origin of that

Chinese expression. One is about two poets.

Zhao Gu was a well-known Tang Dynasty (AD 618-907) poet. People of his time loved his poems. Even today, many poetry buffs can recite verses from Zhao's poems.

During the same time, there was another poet with the name of Chang Jian. Chang was less gifted and could only write second-rate poems, but he was a fan of Zhao and wanted very much to meet his idol.

One day, he was told that Zhao was travelling in Hangzhou, Chang hurried to a big temple in the city because he believed that no tourist would ever exclude the site from his itinerary. To attract Zhao's attention, Chang wrote several unfinished poems on the temple wall. His trick worked. When Zhao saw these unfinished poems, he stopped and added several lines to them to make them complete.

Since Chang's lines were eminently poor and Zhao's verses were graceful and stylish, people said Chang had cast a brick to attract jade.

The saying *Pao Zhuan Yin Yu* is still widely used by Chinese-speakers to express modesty. Often used in spoken or written introductions, the phrase is cited to mean that the introductory remarks are commonplace words offered so others can provide their more valuable opinions or comments.

破 釜 沉 舟

pò　　fū　　chén　　zhōu

To Sink the Boats

In ancient China, when troops were ordered to *Po Fu Chen Zhou* (break the cooking pots and sink the boats after crossing the river), every soldier understood that the battle was one of life or death. Since all means of retreat were cut off, the army had to fight the enemy with all its might or it would face defeat and certain death.

As the legend goes, this was a strategem first employed by a famous rebel leader, Xiang Yu, in 207 BC when he fought a decisive

battle against troops of the Qin Dynasty (221-206 BC).

This year witnessed the first large-scale peasant rebellion in Chinese history. Xiang Yu, a descendant of a noble family, had joined the rebels and became the deputy-commander-in-chief of a rebel army.

One day, the army was ordered to attack Qin troops near the Zhang River in North China. But, the commander in chief, Song Yi, refused to launch the assault fearing that the rebels couldn't hold their own against the well-trained Qin soldiers.

After a 46-day standoff, the rebels began to complain loudly because the weather and other conditions had become increasingly harsh.

Xiang Yu decided to take matters into his own hands. He killed Song Yi and took over control of the army. He brought his men across the Zhang River and then ordered them to break their cooking pots and sink their boats.

Xiang told the rebel army: "Now, we have no means of treat. To survive, you must wipe out the enemy!"

Desperate, the rebels charged the enemy positions and killed thousands of Qin soldiers. As a result, Xiang's army won a decisive battle, which contributed to the final collapse of the Qin Dynasty.

Since then, this tactic has been employed by many other military leaders in Chinese history. And today, *Po Fu Chen Zhou* has become an idiom which has both commendatory and derogatory meanings. It can be used to describe either a person's firm determination to achieve his or her goals or someone who has become desperate in the face of defeat.

旗 鼓 相 当

qí　　gǔ　　xiāng　dāng

Flags and Drums

In the absence of modern equipment such as computers and telecommunication facilities, flags and drums played a key role in directing troops in field battles in ancient China.

Flags of different colours were used to conduct communication and the deploying of troops in battle formations while the drums served as an instrument to boost soldiers' morale and to issue

movement orders.

So, it was natural that the two instruments found their way into a number of Chinese sayings and expressions.

Of those which are still widely quoted is the idiom *Qi Gu Xiang Dang* or "having the same number of flags and drums".

This originates from a letter written by Emperor Guangwu during the early years of Eastern Han Dynasty (AD 25-220). At that time, the new regime was facing strong opposition in remote provinces. Gongsun Shu named himself "emperor" in today's Sichuan Province and Wei Xiao set up a rebel army in the bordering Longxi Area.

Besides opposing the court, the two rebel factions were also involved in deep border disputes with each other.

Emperor Guangwu, who had long planned to take advantage of the brawl between Gongsun and Wei to alleviate opposition pressure in the northwest and southwest provinces, one day wrote a letter to Wei, proposing an alliance against Gongsun.

In the letter the emperor said: "At present, most of the royal troops are fighting rebels in the east. So, I do not have a large number of contingents to be deployed in the west."

"But, if Gongsun Shu launches invasions into any of the central provinces, he will definitely first try to seize the area now under your command. Therefore, I believe that only by forming an alliance between us could we have the same number of flags and drums as Gongsun does."

Wei accepted the emperor's proposal and an anti-Gongsun alliance was soon established.

In the following years, the alliance had not only undermined Gongsun's plans of invading into the central provinces, but also made a number of successful offenses against the military positions of the self-enthroned "emperor".

Today, Chinese people tend to cite the idiom *Qi Gu Xiang Dang* to indicate that someone is a match for another or that it is "horse and horse" between two rival teams.

骑　虎　难　下
qí　hǔ　nán　xià

Riding a Tiger

The popular Chinese idiom *Qi Hu Nan Xia*, or "he who rides a tiger finds it hard to get off", is believed to have originated at the beginning of the Eastern Jin Dynasty (AD 317-420).

When it was first used, it was so apt that it helped extend the rule of the fledgling dynasty for nearly a century.

When Sima Shao, emperor of the newly founded Eastern Jin Dynasty died in AD 325, his young son Sima Yan became the ruler.

But soon after, one of his generals, Su Jun, decided to rebel against him.

In the spring of 328, troops led by General Su launched a surprise attack and soon seized the capital, today's Nanjing in East China. Su killed many officials who were loyal to the court and put the young emperor and empress under house arrest.

When news of the fall of the capital reached central China's Wuchang, Governor Wen Jiao vowed to put down the rebellion and help reinstate the emperor. Wen decided to form an anti-rebel coalition by joining forces with Tao Kan, the governor of Jingzhou.

At first, Tao was reluctant to co-operate with Governor Wen because he was unhappy that the new ruler had never offered him a promotion. But after he learned that his own son had been killed by the rebels in the capital, the governor resolved to join.

The war between those loyal to the court and the rebels lasted for several months and the siege of the capital gradually became a stalemate. Again, Tao hesitated. One day, he told Governor Wen that he intended to quit the war "temporarily" and withdraw his troops to Jingzhou.

Wen immediately warned him of the serious consequences this action would have. He said, "Governor Tao, you should realize that we cannot back down. We are now riding a tiger and it's hard to dismount. If you quit now, the anti-rebel united front may collapse. But, if one day the emperor regains his power, everyone in the court will then point his finger at you!"

Again, the shilly-shallying Tao was won over. The two governors then stayed up all night discussing new military plans. Thanks to their renewed determination and improved tactics, the forces loyal to the court finally defeated the rebels. The rule of the Eastern Jin Dynasty continued for another 92 years.

Today, Chinese people often cite the idiom *Qi Hu Nan Xia* to describe someone who is in a difficult situation but still must carry on.

歧 路 亡 羊
qí　lù　wáng　yáng

Going Astray

A lost lamb isn't much of a story. But the particular one lost more than 2,000 years ago was different. It has not only led to a thought-provoking theorization, but also a popular Chinese idiom, *Qi Lu Wang Yang* or "a lamb going astray in forked roads".

Yang Zi was a famous thinker during the Warring States Period (475-221 BC). One day, one of his neighbours came to him to ask for help.

He told the philosopher one of his lambs was lost and he had already mobilized all his kin to look for it. However, there were still not enough hands. So, he had come to ask Yang to send some of his servants to join the searchers.

Yang felt puzzled and asked: "Why should you need so many people to track down a single lamb?"

The neighbour answered: "Because there are so many forked paths."

After a long time, the searchers including Yang's servants came back empty-handed.

Yang again asked his neighbour: "How could you fail to find the lamb despite so many helping hands?"

"There are just too many branched roads in each forked road."

After hearing the answer, the philosopher became lost in reverie and looked distraught.

One of his students asked: "Sir, why are you concerned about a lamb which isn't worth much and which isn't yours?"

The teacher said that was not the question. He explained the lamb got lost because there were too many forked roads. Similarly, a student could end up nowhere if he could not pick one out of the too many courses of study available and keep to it.

"The conclusion is: One tends to get lost not because there is no path in front of him but there are too many," the thinker commented.

Now, the Chinese saying *Qi Lu Wang Yang* and the story behind it are often quoted to persuade people to devote themselves wholeheartedly to a chosen cause.

杞 人 忧 天
qǐ   rén   yōu   tiān

A Care-Laden Man

Everyone has something to worry about. Their job, family, the protection of the environment or the survival of wildlife. Most worries are fully justified, but others could be imaginary or groundless.

A good example is the popular Chinese saying *Qi Ren You Tian* or "the man of Qi who fears that the sky might fall down".

The story behind the saying dates back to the Zhou Dynasty more than 3,000 years ago.

It says there was a man living in the State of Qi. He was haunted by the fear that some day, the sky might fall down and the earth might collapse.

He was so mentally tortured by this morbid anxiety that he could not eat or sleep in peace.

One of his friends was worried that the man could be driven insane by his imaginary apprehension so decided to have a talk with the man.

"You need not to worry about the sky which is but a mass of air," the friend told the man. "There is air everywhere and we are all surrounded by air.

"Every second, we inhale and exhale the air and we always move around in the air. So, the sky's falling is never likely to happen."

"Okay, maybe you are right. But how about the earth? If the earth collapses, what should I do about it? And then I might have no place to live," the man said.

The friend explained that the earth was made up of huge masses of soil and rock. They extended to every corner and there was no place where there were no such masses.

In addition, people walked, lived and worked on such masses everyday. Therefore, the collapse of the earth was simply impossible.

Thanks to the friend's earnest words and good intention, the man was finally convinced that his fear about the sky's falling and the earth's collapsing was unnecessary. After the conversation, he began to lead a normal life again.

Hearing the news, the friend was very much relieved, too.

Today, the idiom *Qi Ren You Tian* is often cited to describe anyone who entertains unwarranted anxiety.

千 万 买 邻
qiān wàn mǎi lín

A Valuable Neighbour

How much should a good neighbour be worth? Ten million dollars? At least this is what a popular Chinese idiom will tell you.

Qian Wan Mai Lin or "spending 10 million to buy a good neighbour" is one of many Chinese sayings highlighting a long Chinese tradition of valuing an ideal neighbourhood.

For instance, when the ancient Chinese sage, Mencius, was young,

his mother moved their family home three times to find a neighbourhood which she believed would be a beneficial influence on her son.

But *Qian Wan Mai Lin* is perhaps the only Chinese saying that puts a price tag on a good neighbour.

The expression comes from a story about an upright official living some 15 centuries ago.

Lu Sengzhen helped General Xiao Yan establish the Liang Dynasty (AD 502-557). Although Lu was later promoted to a very high position in the imperial court, he remained an official with integrity.

After serving in the court for a couple of years, Lu asked the emperor to allow him to go back to his hometown in East China and so he was appointed the position of local prefectural governor.

In his hometown, the official did everything possible to keep a clean government. He repeatedly declined requests made by his relatives for favours. But he took good care of his neighbours.

One day, a new neighbour moved in. Lu immediately paid a courtesy visit to this new neighbour.

During their conversation, the official asked how much the house cost. The new neighbour said,"11 million".

"What?" Lu said, incredulously, "11 million? How could it be so costly?"

"Oh, no, the house didn't cost much. I spent only 1 million for the house."

"Then, what about the 10 million?"

"That's the value of finding a good neighbour like you," answered the new neighbour.

Even today, Chinese people, still place a higher value on a good, close neighbour, even more than a kinsfolk living far away.

黔　驴　技　穷

qián　　lú　　jì　　qióng

The Guizhou Donkey

Many expressions in the Chinese language can be used to describe something that is formidable in appearance only.

Mao Zedong, for instance, once likened reactionaries and the atom bomb to "paper tigers".

Along with "paper tiger," an idiom about a Guizhou donkey is also frequently cited to describe something that is not as powerful as it seems.

The idiom *Qian Lü Ji Qiong*, or "the Guizhou donkey has exhausted his tricks", is based on a story about a tiger and a donkey.

In ancient times, the story goes, there were no donkeys in Guizh-

ou, now a province in Southwest China. One day, however, after travelling to other provinces around the country, a local folk brought back home a donkey. Since he did not know how to use the animal, he decided to let it roam and graze in some nearby woods.

The newcomer, with its long legs, large ears, black hair and big eyes, almost frightened a tiger living in the woods out of its wits. The tiger thought the donkey must be a divine animal sent by a god. So it hid in thick bushes and dared only occasionally take a quick peep at the interloper.

Out of curiosity, the tiger decided several days later to move a bit closer to get a better look at the donkey. But suddenly, the donkey let out a thundering bray, which made the tiger flee for its life.

Only when the tiger became used to the donkey's loud braying did it dare take another look at the mysterious animal.

After long observation, the tiger decided that the donkey did not look as fearsome as it first did. So the tiger became bolder and bolder with each passing day. One day, it even stood only a few yards away, to make a careful study of the donkey. But still the tiger did not dare make a move.

To find out what weapons the donkey had in its arsenal, the tiger one day came out to tease the donkey. The donkey was angered and gave the tiger a kick. The tiger was greatly relieved.

It then wasted no more time and jumped on to the donkey, which turned into the most delicious dinner the tiger had ever had.

The expressions "paper tiger" and *Qian Lü Ji Qiong* are but two of a number of Chinese expressions for describing something outwardly strong and inwardly weak.

However, the two are different in a way. Perhaps it would be a good idea to think of an atom bomb as a "paper tiger" only before it explodes—and a Guizhou donkey as a weakling only after it explodes.

强 弩 之 末

qiáng　nǔ　zhī　mò

A Powerful Crossbow

"Avoid the enemy when he is full of vigour, strike when he is fatigued and withdraws," said Sun Zi, a famous Chinese strategist, whose works have been read by many military leaders around the world.

This advice by Sun, who lived during the 5th century BC, is

reflected in a number of Chinese sayings and idioms. *Qiang Nu Zhi Mo*, or "a spent arrow shot from a powerful crossbow", is one example.

Like many other Chinese expressions, this idiom originates in a story about war.

During the early years of the Western Han Dynasty (206 BC-AD 24), the nomadic Huns constantly intruded into northern border areas to plunder villages and kill innocent people. Liu Bang, the first emperor of the Western Han, sent thousands of troops to fight the Huns, to no avail.

In 200 BC, Liu personally led a large army to attack the enemy. He failed to defeat them again. This was partly because the new nation was then still very poor and weak.

In the following 50 years, fighting on the northern border continued, bringing great misery to local people.

It was not until the reign of the Emperor Wu, a statesman with rare gifts and bold strategy, that the nation became prosperous and powerful. The Emperor Wu determined to resolve the northern border disputes by launching a series of new crusades against the Huns. Most court officials supported the emperor's plan. But there was one, Han An'guo, who was strongly against it.

Han told the emperor: "Today, we are quite strong. But everyone knows that after travelling a long distance, a strong gust of wind will deteriorate into a tiny breath of air that can hardly ruffle the feathers of a bird; and a spent arrow, though shot from a powerful crossbow, cannot even get through a piece of thin silk.

"The same is true of armies. After our royal troops travel thousands of miles to the northern border, they will never be able to defeat the Huns."

Although the Emperor Wu turned a deaf ear to Han's advice, the truth revealed in the outspoken official's remarks has since been expressed in the popular idiom *Qiang Nu Zhi Mo*.

Today, Chinese people often use this expression to say that any force, no matter how strong at the beginning, will eventually become exhausted over a span of distance or time.

Therefore, to beat your enemy, you must "strike when he is fatigued and withdraws."

青 云 直 上

qīng　yún　zhí　shàng

Meteoric Rise

"Rocket cadre" was a special term used during the "cultural revolution" (1966-76) in China to describe anyone who was rapidly promoted to a high official position.

Today, however, the phrase has become antiquated and people have gone back to the traditional saying, *Qing Yun Zhi Shang* or "a direct rise into the blue sky" to indicate someone who has made a meteoric rise in their career.

The traditional expression was first used during the Warring States Period (475-221 BC).

Fan Ju was an official in the imperial court of the State of Wei. Once, Fan accompanied his patron on a mission to the State of Qi.

The Qi ruler had learned that Fan was an outstanding strategist and elocutionist. So, he sent someone to persuade Fan to stay in his state and work for him. But Fan declined.

However, after returning to the State of Wei, Fan was brutally punished and put into confinement by his patron who suspected that the hanger-on had betrayed him and the State of Wei.

With help from his friends, Fan later fled the State of Wei. He changed his name and went to settle down in the State of Qin.

The Duke of Qin also greatly appreciated the talents of Fan and soon appointed him the prime minister in his court.

Several years later, the State of Qin decided to invade into the State of Wei. So, Fan's original patron was sent by the Wei ruler as a special envoy to the State of Qin to negotiate a peace accord.

The envoy was flabbergasted when he saw his former protege sitting at the other end of the negotiation table as the prime minister of the rival state.

When he finally found his tongue, the envoy began to apologize profusely to Fan for what he did to him a few years ago.

"I didn't expect you would have had such a direct rise into the blue sky," said the envoy.

Fan didn't accept his apology right away. But after giving him a lecture, Fan forgave his former patron and allowed him to go back to the State of Wei.

Today, few Chinese speakers could remember the name of the Wei official, but his phrase *Qing Yun Zhi Shang* remains one of the most quoted sayings in the Chinese language.

请 君 入 瓮

qǐng　jūn　rù　wèng

Hot Vat

One must accept the repercussions of one's acts. That is why Westerners say: "You've made your bed and you must lie on it."

Among Chinese, a similar view is expressed with the idiom *Qing Jun Ru Weng*, or, "Please step into the vat of your own creation".

The vat in the idiom is no ordinary container. It was an instru-

ment of torture thought up by Zhou Xing, an official in the court of the Empress Wu Zetian, during the Tang Dynasty (AD 618-907).

After dethroning her own son, the Emperor Zhongzong, Wu ruled the country for 22 years by means of bloody suppression.

In her court, she employed a group of cruel and oppressive officials. Among them, Lai Junchen, Qiu Shenji and Zhou Xing were the most notorious.

They invented a large number of instruments to torture those they suspected of opposition to the empress, and to force prisoners to admit to crimes. In addition, they put almost every official in the court under secret surveillance.

One day, the Empress Wu summoned Lai Junchen and told him that according to secret reports Qiu Shenji and Zhou Xing were conspiring against the state. The empress then ordered Lai to put Zhou on trial.

Instead of having Zhou arrested, Lai invited him to dinner and, over wine, discussed criminal cases with him. After emptying a few glasses, Lai said:

"Nowadays, I find it very difficult to make some prisoners confess their crimes even after putting them through all kinds of torture. My friend, do you have any ideas on how to deal with them?"

"Very simple," Zhou replied. "Set up a large vat and heat it with charcoal. Then order the prisoner to step into the vat and, believe me, he will confess anything and everything."

At this, Lai ordered soldiers to bring in a large vat and heat it in the way Zhou had just described. When the vat was burning hot, Lai stood up and, with a stern face, told Zhou:

"I have received an imperial order to put you on trial on charges of subversion and conspiracy. Now, my friend, please step into the vat of your own creation."

Instantly, the effects of wine vanished from Zhou's head and cold sweat rolled down his face.

Zhou kowtowed to Lai and pleaded guilty.

Eventually, the three notorious courtiers, hated by so many people, all died in disgrace.

Today, the idiom *Qing Jun Ru Weng* is often cited sarcastically to describe a situation in which, a person is asked to try what he has thought up to use against others.

罄 竹 难 书
qìng　zhú　nán　shū

No Enough Bamboo

Before Cai Lun invented the technology to make paper in AD 105, the ancient Chinese had tried many other materials as surfaces for writing, including bones, tortoise shells and silk.

Of them all, bamboo was most widely used, and for nearly 1,000 years. Naturally, this treelike grass, which flourishes in East and South China, has found its way into Chinese sayings.

Today, one of the most popular Chinese idioms related to bamboo is *Qing Zhu Nan Shu*—or, literally, "all the bamboo, difficult to write".

This expression was first used to mean that even if you could cut

down all the bamboo grown in the ancient Chu and Yue areas and use it for writing, you still won't have enough space to record the crimes committed by Wang Mang, who lived during the Western Han Dynasty (206BC–AD24).

In the late years of the Western Han Dynasty, Wang poisoned the Emperor Pingdi to death, and then he ushered in the Xin Dynasty (AD8–23), naming himself its first emperor. After seizing power, Wang promulgated a series of unpopular policies to increase state revenues. He spent a lot of the money from state coffers on extravagant temples and luxurious palaces for his own family. In addition, he launched a number of bloody wars to suppress minority people living in remote areas.

Wang's brutal rule soon triggered loud cries of discontent all around the country. Thousands of desperate peasants and even his own troops began to rebel against him. In a public denunciation of Wang, a rebel general first used the expression *Qing Zhu Nan Shu* to indicate that the usurper's crimes were too numerous to record. He called on the whole nation to support the rebel forces in overthrowing the Xin Dynasty.

In AD 23, rebel peasants overran Chang'an (today's Xi'an in Shaanxi Province), capital of the Xin Dynasty, and stabbed the self-crowned emperor to death. This proved to be one of many crucial turning points in Chinese history.

Today, although most Chinese use paper or even electronic devices for writing, they still cite the idiom associated to bamboo to describe any multitude of crimes committed by an individual or a group of people.

人 杰 地 灵

rén　jié　dì　líng

A Great Place

Wang Bo (AD 650-676) was one of the "Four Top Scholars" of the early Tang Dynasty. He left behind an archive of literary gems that included prose, verses and expressions that are still widely quoted today.

Ren Jie Di Ling or "a glorious place propitious for giving birth to great men" is but one of those jewels.

On the day of the Double Ninth Festival (9th day of the 9th lunar

month) in AD 675, Wang was invited to a party held in the Tengwangge, a famous pavilion in today's Jiangxi Province.

The participants were mostly local scholars.

After a few rounds of toasts, the host proposed that all the guests write a verse about the pavilion, and the best one would be carved on a stone tablet and erected in front of the building.

Either because of modesty or fear of showing their lack of creativity in front of their peers, none of the guests picked up the brush. The paper, ink and brush were eventually passed onto the table in front of Wang.

The pundits were very surprised to see Wang, the youngest among them, pick up the brush and begin to write a few verses on the paper.

As Wang wrote, some of the guests said his beginning was not exceptional.

But as they read on, they were awed by Wang's gift at creating beautiful stanzas and handsome compositions.

Wang jotted many idioms, including *Ren Jie Di Ling*, to praise the place where the pavilion was located.

When the essay was finished, the host and guests offered Wang their sincere congratulations.

Since then, Wang's article about Tengwangge has been deemed as masterpiece in Chinese literature, and the saying *Ren Jie Di Ling* remains popular idiom in the Chinese language.

塞　翁　失　马
sài　wēng　shī　mǎ

A Lost Mare

Some Chinese idioms are actually expressions of the dialectical thinking of the ancient Chinese.

Many of them believed in the relativity of things and the transformation of two opposite factors. The idiom *Sai Weng Shi Ma*, or "when the old man on the frontier lost his mare", is a good example.

The idiom originates in the Writings of Prince Huainan, which was compiled by a group of thinkers during the Western Han Dynasty (206 BC-AD 24).

The story goes like this:

Long ago, there was a young man living near the Great Wall. He had a mare. One day, his mare fled into an area ruled by tribes of minority nationalities. On learning this, his friends and relatives came to console him. However, his father told him: "Cheer up, son. Who says this may not be a blessing?"

Several months later, the mare came back along with a group of fine horses. The friends and relatives were just as happy as the young man and they all came to congratulate him. But this time, the old man warned his son, saying: "Who says this won't turn out to be a misfortune?"

The young man loved the new horses, and every morning he took a ride on one of them. Since the new horses were not well tamed, the young man fell off one of them one day and became crippled. Again, his friends and relatives came to console him and again the father said: "Who says this may not be a blessing in disguise?"

One year later, the minority tribes began to invade into areas inside the Great Wall. Most young people living in the frontier regions were drafted into the army to fight the invaders. And about nine out of every ten of the draftees later were killed in battle. As a cripple, the owner of the mare was not ordered to join the army and, together with his father, survived the border war.

"Therefore, a blessing may turn out to be a misfortune and the contrary may also be true," the story in the Writings of Prince Huainan concludes.

In the idiom, instead of his son, the old man has become the owner of the mare. And the idiomatic saying is usually followed by the phrase *An Zhi Fei Fu*, meaning, "Who could have guessed it was a blessing in disguise?" Now, *Sai Weng Shi Ma, An Zhi Fei Fu* (When the old man on the frontier lost his mare, who could have guessed it was a blessing in disguise?) is frequently cited by people when they try to console someone who has suffered an unexpected loss or mishap.

三　顾　茅　庐
sān　gù　máo　lú

Visiting the Thatched Cottage

In Chinese literature, there are many stories about the Three Kingdoms (AD 220-280) era. Among them, the story called *San Gu Mao Lu* or "making three calls at the thatched cottage" is one of the best.

Before becoming the ruler of the Kingdom of Shu, Liu Bei tried very hard to find talented people to help him in cause of unifying

China.

One day, when he learned that there was a highly-gifted strategist by the name of Zhuge Liang living in seclusion in a place called Longzhong, Liu decided to make a call at his thatched cottage.

After Liu and two of his best friends got there, they were told by Zhuge's houseboy that the scholar was away for several weeks. Very disappointed, they left.

A few months later, Liu and his friends came to Zhuge's cottage again in a heavy snowstorm. But once again, they were told Zhuge was not at home and probably would not be back for couple of days.

After the two failed calls, Liu's friends tried to persuade him to give up his endeavour. One of them said: "Zhuge is impolite for not making a returned call. Maybe, he is but another pedant living in the countryside."

Liu replied: "At present, I need very much all kinds of talented people to support my cause. I will not give up my efforts. If you don't want to go, I'll go myself. I believe Zhuge will be moved by my sincerity."

When Liu went to Longzhong for the third time, he was met by Zhuge personally at the entrance of the village.

The two had a long discussion on the military situation in China and made a long-term plan to unify the country.

Later, Zhuge became the top military adviser and prime minister for Liu's regime.

Nowadays, the title of the story, *San Gu Mao Lu*, has become a widely-quoted idiom. It is used to refer to a potentate who repeatedly requests someone to take up a responsible post.

三 人 成 虎

sān rén chéng hǔ

Man-made Tigers

A lie, if repeated often enough, will be accepted as truth. Chinese often cite the idiom *San Ren Cheng Hu* or "three men make a tiger" to illustrate this idea.

The expression was first quoted by Pang Cong, an official in the State of Wei during the Warring States Period (475-221 BC).

The State of Wei signed an agreement with the State of Zhao to form an alliance. As was the custom at the time, the Wei king had

to send his son as a hostage for a set term to the State of Zhao in order to minimize suspicion between the two sides. Pang Cong was selected to go with the prince.

Before departure, Pang asked the king: "If someone reported to Your Highness that a tiger was loose in the market, would you believe him?"

"Of course, I wouldn't," the king answered.

"If a second man came to tell you that a tiger was loose in the street, would you believe it then?" Pang pressed.

"I might start wondering about it," the king replied.

Pang continued, "If a third man came to report news of a tiger in the street, then would you finally buy it?" he asked.

After pondering for a moment, the king said: "Yes, I'd probably believe it."

Pang told the king that after he left for the State of Zhao there might be more than three people talking him down behind his back. He hoped that the king would make his own judgement without influenced by others.

The king said: "Don't worry. I trust you and I know how to make my own judgements."

After Pang left, several of his colleagues began slandering him in front of the king. Eventually the king became suspicious of Pang's loyalty.

When Pang returned with the prince after serving the hostage term, he found himself in disfavour.

Nowadays, Pang's idiom invoking "tigers" is used to warn people against listening to liars.

死 灰 复 燃

sǐ   huī   fù   rán

Dead Ashes Flare up

Life is hard to predict. Sometimes, a seemingly set course can take sharp turns. One popular Chinese saying implying such unpredictability is *Si Hui Fu Ran* or "dead ashes flare up again".

The phrase was first coined by Han An'guo, an official who lived during the Han Dynasty (206 BC-AD 220).

Han became a favourite aide of King Liang Xiao after he helped suppress a major military revolt. However, Han was later accused of violating imperial laws by rival officials and put into jail in Mengxian county.

The local magistrate was a vicious man. He thought Han had fallen into disgrace and would never be reinstated in the court. So, he often came to see Han and make fun of him.

Han, of course, was very angry. One day, Han told the magistrate, "You see me as dead ashes. But are you sure that the dead ashes will never flare up again?"

"No, I'm not," answered the magistrate. "But if the dead ashes do flare up. I'll piss them out."

Han was deeply insulted, but he could do nothing about it at the moment.

Some years later, King Liang Xiao found an opportunity to free Han and appointed him one of his top ministers.

Learning about the news, the Mengxian county magistrate deserted his office and fled to a remote area, fearing that Han would take revenge for the mistreatment he received in Mengxian prison.

After Han spread the word that he might kill all the magistrate's kin if the official didn't turn himself in, the former county chief surrendered himself to Han.

Han recalled their conversation in Mengxian prison and asked the magistrate: "Now, you see the dead ashes are glowing again. Why don't you piss on them?"

The magistrate was so frightened that he kept kowtowing and begging Han to pardon him.

Han told the magistrate to mend his ways and let him go.

Today, the expression *Si Hui Fu Ran* has a derogatory connotation. It often indicates the resurgence of some dying evil forces.

四 面 楚 歌

sì　　miàn　　chǔ　　gē

Mournful Songs

Most Chinese like the mellow and touching folk songs from the south. But few want to hear them "on all sides". This is because of the popular idiom *Si Mian Chu Ge* or "hearing the Chu songs on all sides".

This expression comes from the last battle fought by Xiang Yu, a famous general of a rebel army, more than 2,000 years ago.

Following the peasants' uprisings of the Qin Dynasty (221-206 BC), Xiang Yu and Liu Bang, another rebel army commander,

began fighting each other for the reign of the country. Since most soldiers of Xiang's army, including Xiang himself, came from the Chu area (today's East China), it was called the Chu Army. Its rival was the Han Army.

After several defeats, the Chu Army had retreated to a place named Gaixia, where it was surrounded by the enemy on all sides. In a few days, the Chu soldiers found their food supply was running out. Xiang tried a couple times to break the siege, but failed.

One night, as Xiang was sitting in his tent, he began to hear songs from the Chu area flowing in on all sides. He came out and found that it was the Han soldiers who were all loudly singing the Chu songs. The general wondered how the rival army could have recruited so many soldiers who were able to sing Chu songs. But he also wondered if his enemy might not have already captured the Chu area.

In truth, it was a psychological trick conjured up by Liu's advisers and the scheme worked. Hearing the familiar tunes from their home areas, most of the men in the Chu Army became nostalgic and some even began to sing along and weep. By midnight, more than half of Xiang's men had deserted.

The next morning, Xiang made his last attempt to break the siege. By the time he finally reached the Wujiang River, less than a dozen people remained out of his 8,000 man army. The humiliated general drew his sword and cut his own throat.

Today the saying *Si Mian Chu Ge* is frequently used to describe anyone exposed to attacks from all sides, or one who has been driven to the wall. So there are not many people in China who would like hearing the melodious Chu tunes from "all sides".

守 口 如 瓶

shǒu　kǒu　rú　píng

Tight-lipped

To excel in the official circle, one must follow some rules. According to a high-ranking official in the Northern Song Dynasty, the most important rule is *Shou Kou Ru Ping* or "to keep your mouth as tight as a jar lid".

Fu Bi was a highly-gifted young man when he first met Fan Zhongyan, a famous scholar in Chinese history. Fan appreciated Fu's talent and learning and recommended this young man to the

minister in charge of military affairs in the imperial court.

Soon, Fu married the daughter of the minister and was appointed by the emperor as a county judge.

Later on, he rose meteorically to the post of prime minister in the imperial court.

However, Fu did not see eye to eye with his colleague Wang Anshi, a well-known reformist of that time. He knew that Wang would someday replace him as the prime minister, but he never talked about it to anyone.

One day, the emperor asked Fu who he would recommend as his successor in the future. Fu mentioned the name of an official other than Wang. The emperor did not make any comment.

Then the emperor asked whether Fu would agree to having Wang as his successor. This time, Fu failed to reply. So, the monarch immediately realized that Fu and Wang did not get along.

When Wang began to push ahead his bold rural economic reform programme, Fu resigned from his post and went to live in his home village in Henan.

Despite the fact that he had already left the court, Fu kept writing to the emperor making proposals and airing frank comments on state affairs. And the emperor, though not always following Fu's advice, always spoke highly of his former aide.

Some friends once asked Fu what was the most important rule that one must follow in pursuing a political career like his. Fu said: "You should keep your mouth as tight as a jar lid."

Today, Fu's expression, *Shou Kou Ru Ping* has become a very popular Chinese idiom. People often quote it to describe someone who is tight-lipped or who breathes not a single word about a secret.

守 株 待 兔
shǒu　zhū　dài　tù

Hare-brained

Although almost everyone has heard of the old saying "No pains, no gains", there still are many who trust to chance or wait for windfalls. Chinese speakers often use the idiom, *Shou Zhu Dai Tu*, or "standing by a tree stump, waiting for a hare to crash into it", to describe such a person.

The saying originated long, long ago, in the State of Song.

One day, the story goes, a farmer was labouring in the fields when

he saw a hare running past him, dashing itself into a tree stump a few yards away. The hare passed out immediately upon impact.

The farmer walked up, picked up the godsent gift of food and was overjoyed. He decided to call it a day, though the sun was still high.

He prepared a tasty dish from the hare for dinner. After a few shots of liquor, he became a little tipsy.

He thought aloud, "If I can pick up one hare a day, I wouldn't ever need to sweat in the fields again. The stump on my plot must be the blessed place to wait for such windfalls."

So, beginning on the next day, the farmer

stopped tending his crops and did nothing but stood by his stump, waiting for more hares to come along and knock themselves out on it.

Several days passed, no hares appeared. Meanwhile, the field was quickly becoming overgrown, and the farmer soon became the laughing stock of the local area.

Today, almost everywhere in the world, one can still find disciples of this Song farmer.

And the saying, *Shou Zhu Dai Tu*, no longer just means someone who waits for gains with no pains, it also carries with it a connotation of being stupid and lacking innovation.

水　滴　石　穿
shuǐ　dī　shí　chuān

Water Power

The power of a single drop of water is, naturally, slight. But, the constant dripping of that water will wear away the hardest stone. This universal truth is crystallized in a popular Chinese saying, *Shui Di Shi Chuan*, meaning, "dripping water wears away the stone".

Few would think though that this saying was first cited as a reason for executing a corrupt Song Dynasty (960-1279) aide.

Zhang Guaiya was the magistrate of Chongyang County. He was reputedly an upright official who hated the widespread corruption in the officialdom at that time.

The magistrate had tried many means to fight wrongful behaviours to establish a clean government in the county, but few were successful.

One day, as he was patrolling near the county government office, the magistrate saw an aide coming out of the office in a hurry. Zhang stopped him and asked him what had happened, but the aide hemmed and hawed.

Then the magistrate spotted a coin hidden behind one of the

aide's ears. When questioned, the aide admitted that the coin had been stolen from the government's office.

The magistrate took the aide immediately into court and decided to punish him. The defendant protested: "I have just stolen only a single coin. There's no reason to make such a fuss."

The aide even went so far as to challenge the magistrate, by saying, "You might punish me by torturing me, but dare you execute me for just stealing a coin?"

But the magistrate said, "Yes, I would. Because if you steal one coin a day, after a thousand days, the money stolen would amount to 1,000 coins. With a single waterdrop a day, constant dripping will wear away the stone."

Upon saying this, the magistrate drew out his own sword and chopped off the aide's head.

The entire court was stunned by what the magistrate did, but the official explained, "I executed him not just for stealing of one coin, but to attempt to stop the widespread corruption in the county." People have differing opinions about the magistrate's action, but the illustration he gave for executing the thief had become a popular Chinese idiom.

Today, the saying *Shui Di Shi Chuan* is used frequently by Chinese speakers to underscore the idea that constant effort brings success.

水 深 火 热
shuǐ　shēn　huǒ　rè

Water and Fire

Few people are likely to survive without water or fire but no-one wants to live in deep water or scorching fire. Mencius, a famous Chinese scholar, obtained a good understanding of this ambivalence more than 2,000 years ago. He created the Chinese idiom *Shui Shen Huo Re* or "deep water and scorching fire" to describe a situation where people suffer deep distress.

During the Warring States Period (475-221 BC), the troops of the

State of Qi invaded the State of Yan by taking advantage of the latter's lingering civil war.

When Qi troops entered the territory of Yan, they were actually welcomed by local residents.

However, a few months later, people in many parts of the State of Yan began to fight the invaders, largely because some Qi officers and soldiers acted indiscreetly and harmed the feelings of the Yan people.

One day, the Qi king invited the visiting scholar Mencius to his court to discuss the issue of the State of Yan.

The king told the scholar some people had suggested Qi annex Yan, while others said Qi troops should withdraw from the Yan as early as possible.

The ruler then asked for the opinion of Mencius.

The scholar said if the Yan people welcomed the annexation, Qi should take over Yan but that if the Yan people were unhappy about the annexation Qi troops should pull out of Yan.

Menicus said: "When the Qi troops first invaded Yan, they were warmly received by local people, which meant they were fed up with the civil war and wished to see someone who could liberate the state.

"However, now it seems the Qi troops have brought great disasters to the Yan people, who do not like the idea of permanent occupation by Qi troops. So, Your Excellency would better order the withdrawal at an earlier date.

"This is because although everyone needs water and fire no-one wants to live in deep water or scorching fire. If the Yan people are made to suffer they will look for other liberators, just as they did with the Qi troops."

Unfortunately, the scholar's advice fell on the deaf ears. The king of the State of Qi gave the go-ahead for the plan of annexing the State of Yan. Yet in the face of the strong resistance put up by the Yan people, who were supported by other states, the Qi troops had to withdraw from Yan territory several months later.

Nowadays *Shui Shen Huo Re*, the wise saying created by Mencius, is often quoted by people to describe anyone who is living in an abyss of suffering.

太 公 钓 鱼
tài　gōng　diào　yú

Hook, Line and Sinker

An old man with a long white beard is angling on a river. He holds a rod with a hookless and baitless line three feet above the water. When asked how could he expect to net any fish with such angling gear, the old man says: "The fish that is destined to be caught will come up."

This is the scene witnessed more than 3,000 years ago on the Weishui River in northwest China. Several days later the old man, called Jiang Shang, did catch something but it was not a fish. It was a king.

Today, it is widely believed that this is the story behind the

popular Chinese idiom *Tai Gong Diao Yu* (Jiang Tai Gong's angling). Originally a trick designed by Jiang to draw attention, the idiom now means that a willing victim will let himself be caught.

Once an official in the court of the Shang Dynasty (16th century-11th century BC), Jiang later quit his post because he foresaw the collapse of the regime, which was plagued by widespread corruption. Despite his advanced age, Jiang still wished to serve a "sagacious" ruler.

Therefore, he designed a bizarre way of fishing in order to attract attention from King Wen of the Western Zhou Dynasty (11th century-771 BC), who was then seeking worthy persons to help him overthrow the Shang Dynasty.

Jiang's trick worked. After angling on the Weishui River for three days, the story about a "stupid old man" fishing in a bizarre manner was heard by the king. When learning the background of the "stupid old man", the king was convinced that Jiang was a person with brilliant talent.

Next day, the king personally went to see the old man on the river. However, Jiang first declined to talk to the king because he thought him lacking in sincerity. When the king came back again three days later, the two reached an agreement and by brushing aside opposition from some of his aides, the king offered Jiang the title of "Tai Gong", a senior position in the court.

Later, Jiang, now better known by his title Tai Gong, helped King Wen and his successor, King Wu, unite the kingdom and overthrow the Shang Dynasty. To cite him for his meritorious service, Jiang was first appointed as the prime minister and later made the Duke of Qi.

Today, when people quote the idiom *Tai Gong Diao Yu*, they are describing some willing victim who is like the "fish rising to Jiang Tai Gong's hookless and baitless line".

贪 生 怕 死
tān shēng pà sǐ

Life and Death

It's natural that most people love life and fear death. But they will call a man a coward if he leads a dishonourable life for fear of death.

In the Chinese language, a popular idiom to this effect is *Tan Sheng Pa Si* or "to covet life and fear death".

The phrase was first used to describe Liu Li, an ill-famed king of the feudal state of Liang during the Han Dynasty (206 BC-AD 220).

After becoming the king of Liang, Liu wielded absolute power and oppressed the people. Upset by his behaviour, many of Liu's aides complained to the imperial court of the Han Dynasty.

At first, the emperor intended to punish Liu. But some of the emperor's advisers said according to Confucius' teachings, nobles should not be punished like common people if they violated imperial laws.

This ritual was designed to protect the reputation of the imperial court and the emperor.

So, instead of penalizing the king, they suggested the emperor ignore the complaints and offer more benefits to the king to show his generosity and tolerance. The emperor agreed.

The king of Liang took the emperor's decision as implied encouragement. As a result, he acted more recklessly than before and cared for no one.

He executed three of his aides in reprisal for their telling the emperor about his being a tyrant. He threw others in jail.

It was not until a new emperor mounted the throne that the imperial court sent several high-ranking officials to Liang to investigate Liu's conduct. The examiners told the king that he might be dethroned if he did not mend his ways.

This time, Liu realized the seriousness of the matter and asked the new emperor for amnesty.

He told the imperial court that he was just a person who coveted life and feared death. However, he did not have any intention to act against the emperor's will.

Like his predecessor, the new emperor forgave Liu and let him escape punishment.

But Heaven refused to forgive the tyrant. Liu eventually committed suicide after becoming embroiled in a power struggle.

Since then, the idiom *Tan Sheng Pa Si* has frequently been quoted to describe anyone who prefers life to honour or who cares nothing but saving his skin.

螳 臂 挡 车
táng   bì   dǎng   chē

The Feeble Praying Mantis

It is always tragic when someone over-estimates himself and attempts in vain to hold back an overwhelmingly superior force.

In China, people often use such idioms as *Pi Fu Han Shu* (an ant trying to topple a tree) or *Tang Bi Dang Che* (a praying mantis trying to stop a chariot) to describe such behaviour.

The latter derives from a story about a well-known ancient Chinese scholar, Yan He.

It was during the late Spring and Autumn Period (770-476 BC). Yan, famous for his scholastic accomplishments, paid a visit to the State of Wei. He was warmly received by Duke Weiling, who asked the scholar to tutor his son, Kuai Kui.

Knowing that Kuai was a young devil who treated human life as if it were not worth a straw, Yan hesitated to accept the duke's offer. Therefore, he went to discuss the matter with his friend Qu Boyu, who was a respected scholar.

Yan told his friend that he was inclined to accept the duke's offer so that he could help change his son's behaviour and prevent him from doing harm to his country and people in the future. "But, if I force him to stop his outrages now, he might take my life. So what should I do?" Yan asked.

Qu did not give the visiting scholar a direct answer. Instead, he told him the following story:

"One day, I was riding a chariot in the countryside. Suddenly, I saw a praying mantis jump into the middle of the road. Wielding its two 'knives', the insect seemed to be trying to stop the vehicle. A moment later, however, the praying mantis was crushed under the wheels of the chariot. Obviously, it was simply impossible for such a feeble insect to stop a running chariot."

"Now," Qu continued, "in my eyes, you are just like that mantis. You overrated yourself when you thought you could mend the ways of the duke's son. You might be put to death by the nortorious young devil before you could do anything to turn him into a kindhearted man."

After listening to the story of *Tang Bi Dang Che*, the visiting scholar decided to take his friend's advice and declined the duke's offer. He even shortened his visit to the State of Wei.

Several years later, the scholar learned that the duke's son had committed numerous crimes and was hated by almost everyone in his country. Finally, the young devil himself was killed by someone else.

螳　螂　捕　蝉
táng　láng　bǔ　chán

A Cicada Story

A cicada, a praying mantis, an oriole and a young man. Can you guess what's special about the four? If not, your Chinese friends will tell you that this peculiar group is responsible for a famous and thought-provoking idiom in the Chinese language.

The story concerning this idiom, *Tang Lang Bu Chan* (a praying mantis stalks a cicada), dates back to the late Spring and Autumn Period (770-476 BC).

After defeating the State of Yue, the king of the State of Wu became arrogant and indulged himself in creature comforts. He was not aware that the king of the State of Yue was undergoing great self-imposed hardships in order to strengthen his resolve to wipe out the humiliation of his defeat.

Wu Zixu, an upright official in the court of the State of Wu, repeatedly warned the king about the potential danger. But the king

turned a deaf ear to the warnings and finally, fed up with Wu Zixu's nagging, he ordered the official to commit suicide.

Meanwhile, the king of Yue was preparing to launch attacks against the State of Wu. Seeing the pending danger, Crown Prince You of the State of Wu decided to use a ploy to convince the king that something must be done to fend off the coming attacks.

One day, the crown prince, with a slingshot in his hand and wet like a drenched chicken, went to see the king of Wu. "What happened to you?" the king asked. The crown prince then told the king the following story:

"When I went into the garden this morning, I saw a cicada was chirping on a tree and a praying mantis was sneakily approaching the insect from behind. As the mantis was about to strike, it didn't notice an oriole waiting for an opportunity for a quick meal.

"I thought the bird did not notice that I was standing under the tree with a slingshot in my hand, so I decided to move step backward and shoot the bird. However, I failed to see that there was a small pond behind me and when I stepped back, I fell in."

After listening to You's story, the king of Wu burst into laughter. "You are stupid. You cared too much about the gains ahead without being aware of the danger behind," the king said. "You must take a lesson from this."

"Yes," the crown prince answered. "But, others should also draw a lesson from my experience."

"What do you mean?" the king asked. The crown prince said that for no reason, the State of Qi invaded the State of Lu, but it did not expect that the State of Wu would attack it from the rear. And now, the State of Wu had become complacent after its victory over the State of Yue, but did not suspect that the latter was preparing to mount an offensive.

The king of Wu angrily interrupted You, saying: "You are playing the same old tune as Wu Zixu did before. I do not want to hear about this any more."

A few years later, the State of Yue's troops launched a mass invasion of the State of Wu and soon seized the whole kingdom. The king of Wu killed himself.

So, when one is so eager to lay his hands on the gains ahead, he should think about this Chinese idiom of a cicada, a praying mantis, an oriole and a young man.

天　罗　地　网
tiān　luó　dì　wǎng

An Escape-proof Net

Many Chinese idioms have survived centuries and still remain popular today simply because of their vivid expression and rich imagination. *Tian Luo Di Wang* or "a sky-size snare and an earth-large net" is one of them.

This saying was first quoted by Wu Yuan, a general who lived during the Spring and Autumn Period (770-476 BC).

Wu Yuan's father was an official in the court of the State of Chu.

However, he was victimized by a scandal in the court when the Chu ruler married a young woman who was originally engaged to the prince.

Fearing the old Wu might blow the whistle, the Chu ruler ordered the execution of the Wu family.

At that time, Wu Yuan was stationed in a remote town. He was warned and told to flee before the killers arrived.

But Wu was outraged to learn his kin weren't as lucky and all had been killed. So, he waited to confront the king's envoy.

The envoy told Wu the king wanted him to go to the court and receive an imperial award. Wu knew it was a trap.

He asked the envoy how his father and family were. The envoy said they all were well.

"You are lying," shouted Wu. "I know you are trying to coax me to step into a sky-size snare and an earth-large net."

Wu beat up the envoy and then escaped to the neighbouring State of Wu.

The Wu king admired Wu Yuan and later promoted him to a high position in his court.

Eventually, Wu Yuan took his revenge on his enemies for the killing of his family.

Now, the expression *Tian Luo Di Wang* is frequently used to mean an escape-proof net or an invisible net that prevents escape.

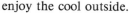

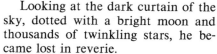

天　衣　无　缝

tiān　yī　wú　fèng

A Heavenly Dress

People say nothing is perfect. But Chinese people think there is. They believe there is one perfect thing in the universe and that is "a heavenly dress without seams"—*Tian Yi Wu Feng*.

This saying came from a dream had by a young man called Guo Han, who lived in a samll village a long, long time ago.

One hot summer night, Guo could not fall asleep, so he came out of the house and sat down on a straw mattress in his courtyard to enjoy the cool outside.

Looking at the dark curtain of the sky, dotted with a bright moon and thousands of twinkling stars, he became lost in reverie.

He thought of the legend about the goddess of the moon and the legendary romance between the cowherd and a lady spinner.

"Now that the pretty woman weaver is living in the heaven, all the colourful clouds we can see at dawn and in the evening must be her works," he thought.

Just then, a cloud in the dark sky metamorphosed before his eyes, and a beautiful young woman gracefully descended into his courtyard.

He could not believe his eyes.

"I must be dreaming," he said to himself, but, he clearly saw the breathtakingly beautiful young woman standing in front of him.

After recovering from his initial shock, the young man asked her, "Are

145

you a goddess from the heaven?"

The woman answered, "I am the woman weaver who appeared in your imagination just a moment ago."

Hardly able to contain his excitement, the young man stared at the divine woman from head to toe, and saw that her dress was truly remarkable, so shapely and, amazingly, sewn without a single seam.

He asked, "Did you make your dress yourself? Why does it have no seams?"

She answered, "Yes, I tailored it. This is a heavenly dress, so it has no seams."

When the young man woke from his dream, the lady spinner was gone, but the next morning, he couldn't wait to tell his amazing story to all his neighbours.

Today, *Tian Yi Wu Feng* has become a popular saying for Chinese-speaking people to use when they want to describe something that is flawless, particularly well-designed plans, or a watertight legal case—these are said to be like a "seamless heavenly dress".

铁 杵 成 针
tiě　chǔ　chéng　zhēn

Iron Rod and Needle

The verbatim tanslation of *Tie Chu Cheng Zhen* is "to grind an iron rod into a needle". This Chinese idiom has a similar meaning as such phrases as "grinding away at one's studies" and "keeping one's nose to the grindstone". But, behind the idiom there is an interesting story about Li Bai, one of the greatest poets in Chinese history.

Born into a rich merchant's family in the Tang Dynasty (AD

618-907), Li was a prodigy when it came to writing Chinese classic poetry. He began to write poems when he was only ten, but, he wasn't a hardworking student and tended to while away his time outdoors.

One day, when Li was roaming through a small village, he saw an old woman grinding an iron rod on a big grindstone in front of a straw-thatched hut. Being curious, the teenager went forward and asked: "What are you doing?" The old woman answered, "Making a needle." "What? Making a needle out of an iron rod?" Li burst into laughter, thinking the old woman must be crazy.

But, the old woman said seriously: "Don't laugh, young man. As long as I keep grinding, I will make a fine needle out of this coarse rod someday." Li stopped laughing and began to ponder on the meaning of the old woman's remark for a quite while. Then, with great respect, he bowed deeply to the needle grinder, turned around and went back home.

After that day, Li became a very diligent student and made *Tie Chu Cheng Zhen* his lifelong motto. Later, he established himself in Chinese literature as a famous poet. Even today, Li's poems enjoy great popularity among Chinese-speaking people all over the world.

And *Tie Chu Cheng Zhen*, a story which has been retold for generations, is now not only a household word in China but also a legend reflecting the Chinese people's deep belief in being industrious.

投　鼠　忌　器
tóu　shǔ　jì　qì

Spare the Rat

The Chinese idiom *Tou Shu Ji Qi* or "hesitate before pelting a rat for fear of smashing the dishes beside it" is nearly the equivalent of the English saying, "burn not your house to rid it of the mouse".

In the Chinese expression, the rat originally meant not the rodent people usually think of, but the high-ranking officials in the imperial court.

The saying was first quoted in an essay "On Government", written by Jia Yi, a famous thinker and writer in the early years of

the Western Han Dynasty (206BC-AD24).

This essay, presented to the emperor of that time by the scholar, touched upon wideranging issues on how to rule the country. In one section, Jia suggested the imperial court adopt a system of feudal rites to consolidate the regime.

Actually, the system meant treating the common people and the nobles under a double standard.

Jia said in the essay that severe punishments should be meted out to ordinary people who violate feudal rites. The corporal punishments suggested by the writer included tattooing one's face with insulting words, cutting off one's nose, chopping off the feet and flogging.

However, these punishments should never be applied to nobles who had violated the feudal rites, even though the emperor might order them to be killed.

Jia explained this was because nobles were a special group of people who were very close to the ruler. If they were punished in the same way as the common people, it would be an insult to the imperial court and damage the image of the emperor.

To illustrate his point, the writer said: "You should hesitate to pelt a rat for fear of smashing the dishes beside it."

Today, the idiom *Tou Shu Ji Qi* is often cited to describe someone who hesitates to take action for fear of hurting innocent people or damaging precious things.

完 璧 归 赵
wán　bì　guī　zhào

Jade Wise

For some Chinese idioms, people are more interested in the stories behind them rather than the sayings themselves. One such example is *Wan Bi Gui Zhao* or "to bring back the jade intact to the State of Zhao".

The jade story dates back to the Warring States Period (475-221 BC).

After learning that King Huiwen of the State of Zhao had acquired an extremely beautiful piece of jade, the ruler of the State Qin sent a letter to the Zhao monarch.

In the letter, the Qin king offered 15 towns to the State of Zhao in exchange for the treasure.

King Huiwen was worried that the Qin king might take the jade from him and then refuse to give him the 15 towns. But, since Qin was much more powerful than Zhao, it seemed that the Zhao ruler had to comply with the request.

So, he decided to appoint Lin Xiangru, a brave and resourceful person, as his envoy to bring the stone to the State of Qin and seal the deal with the Qin king.

Before departure, Lin told the Zhao king that he would bring back the jade intact if the Qin ruler broke his word.

After receiving the stone, the Qin ruler was so pleased. He held it in his hands and showed it to his aides. It seemed that he had forgotten to give the promised towns to Zhao.

Seeing this, the Zhao envoy told the Qin king that the jade had a flaw and would like to show it to him. But when the stone was in his hand, the envoy retreated a few steps to lean on a column threatening to break both the jade and his own head against the column if the king forced him to submit the stone without giving Zhao the promised towns.

The Qin king did not want to see the treasure destroyed, so he agreed to the Zhao envoy's demand, saying he would hold a grand ceremony to exchange the stone.

That night, the envoy sneaked out of the State of Qin and returned the jade intact to the State of Zhao as he had promised.

Today, as a result, the saying *Wan Bi Gui Zhao* is often cited to describe something being returned to its owner intact.

玩　物　喪　志
wán　wù　sàng　zhì

Will-sapping Indulgence

While Chinese people love hobbies, it is a cherished notion that it is best to distance one's self from any indulgence that interferes with career pursuits.

The principle is best expressed in a 3,000-year-old Chinese saying *Wan Wu Sang Zhi* or "indulging in a hobby saps one's will".

The saying was coined by an aide to the first ruler of the Western Zhou Dynasty (11th century-771 BC), which was established after the downfall of the Shang Dynasty (16th century-11th century BC).

The collapse of the Shang Dynasty was caused by the corruption of King Zhou, the last ruler of the regime.

Zhou was a notorious tyrant who indulged himself in material pleasures. He boasted huge collections of precious stones, pearls, exotic plants, as well as rare birds and animals.

He squandered tons of treasury gold on the construction of grandiose palaces and gardens where he spent most of his time playing with his hundreds of concubines and maids of honour. He was so preoccupied with trivial and sensual pursuits that he almost totally ignored his duties as head of state.

Zhou was hated by both his aides and subjects. Eventually, his regime was overthrown and he burned himself to death.

After ascending the throne, King Wu, the new ruler of the Western Zhou Dynasty, found his palace inundated with valuable gifts presented by small neighbouring kingdoms. Many of the gifts were attractive and valuable.

One of the new ruler's aides feared King Wu might follow the same disastrous course as King Zhou. So, one day he came to see the new ruler and reminded him of the failure of his predecessor.

He said indulging in material pleasures or hobbies would sap the king's will to lead his state and people to prosperity. So, he persuaded the ruler to distance himself from any indulgences.

The phrase *Wan Wu Sang Zhi*, cited by the aide to promote moderation, is still popular today. It is often used to warn people that too much attention to extracurricular activities will soften one's determination to achieve more important goals in life.

亡　羊　补　牢
wáng　yáng　bǔ　láo

Tending the Flock

Wang Yang Bu Lao or "to tend the flock after losing sheep" has been regarded as helpful advice in China for more than 2,000 years, probably because often, it is found that it is never too late to take precautions.

The phrase was spoken first by Zhuang Xin, an official at King Xiang's court in the State of Chu during the Warring States Period (475-221 BC).

The king had surrounded himself with four crafty, fawning officials who had won the ruler's deep trust. But none of his gang of four knew anything or ever cared about government and the state affairs.

One day, Zhuang Xin, an upright and outspoken aide, came to see the king and warn him that his regime was collapsing because he had trusted the wrong persons with the job of governing the state.

The king, though, thought Zhuang was jealous of the power and privilege given to the his gang of four. So, he said: "Do you imply that your colleagues are demons?"

Zhuang answered that he did not, "but I predict that they are going to ruin this state very soon."

Failing to persuade the king to distance himself from the evil foursome, Zhuang resigned and moved to a neighbouring state.

About five months later, Chu was invaded by the State of Qin. Soon, the Chu capital was seized by the enemy's army.

Gnawed by deep regret, the king paid a visit to his former official at his residence and asked him for advice on how to recover the lost territories and take back the capital.

Zhuang responded: "According to a popular saying, it is not too late to unleash the hunting dogs after the hare is spotted, and it is not too late to tend the flock even after some of the sheep have been lost.

"As long as Your Excellency trusts the right people and unites the population, a chance to repel the invaders and recover the lost territory remains."

Following Zhuang's advice, the king was able to recover most part of the lost territories in the following months.

Nearly everyone experiences some loss in their lifetime. It is almost unavoidable. What's advisable here is to remember the wisdom of the Chinese idiom *Wang Yang Bu Lao*, and get prepared to tend the flock after those losses occur.

望 梅 止 渴
wàng　méi　zhǐ　kě

Imaginary Plums

When Chinese say that someone is trying to satisfy his or her desire by illusion, they frequently use the phrase *Wang Mei Zhi Ke*. The literal meaning is to quench one's thirst by looking at imaginary fresh plums.

There is a story to this idiom:

Cao Cao was a famous Chinese military strategist and politician in late Eastern Han Dynasty (AD 25-220). One hot summer's day, Cao was leading a large army in a rapid march to launch a surprise attack on the enemy's rear.

However, the scorching summer heat and the heavy armour suits soon drained the soldiers of energy. By noon, thirsty and dripping with sweat, the troops were moving at a snail's pace. It appeared impossible for the army to reach its destination on time.

Meanwhile, the scouts came back and reported to Cao that they could not find any drinking water nearby. The strategist, however, was suddenly struck with an idea. He raced onto the top of a near-by hill and pretended to look carefully ahead in the direction of his destination. Then, he shouted to his soldiers: "There are many plum trees in the valley and all the plums are ripe. They are both sour and sweet, so we can eat some fresh plums to quench our thirst. Come on, men."

Hearing Cao's remarks, the soldiers' mouths began to water and they quickened their pace, rushing towards the valley. But, they were very disappointed when they got to the valley and could not find even a single plum tree. Fortunately, the scouts had discovered a streamlet not far away and had brought back some buckets of cool water.

The army consequently reached its destination on time and launched a successful offensive against the enemy. Having been handed down by the generations, Cao Cao's ploy has now become a household word in China.

危 如 累 卵
wēi　　rú　　lěi　　luǎn

A Pile of Eggs

When a situation is sticky or delicate, the Chinese tend to describe it by quoting the idiom *Wei Ru Lei Luan*, or "as precarious as a pile of eggs". There are a few Chinese expressions associated with eggs, but among them *Wei Ru Lei Luan* is perhaps the most vivid.

The saying was coined by Mei Cheng, a famous writer from the Han Dynasty. Mei once served as an aide to King Liu Pi, ruler of the State of Wu.

After Liu's son was killed during a quarrel with a prince in the

Han imperial court, the king grew to loathe the Han regime.

He frequently feigned illness in order to miss the regular sessions of the imperial court.

Later on, he plotted a rebellion against the Han rule.

Learning this, Mei Cheng immediately came to see the king. Mei told the ruler that under the circumstances at that time, Liu's uprising could never succeed because the Han regime was too strong. Instead, Mei said, it might put the king into a situation as hazardous as eggs piled up.

Mei's prediction was right.

When the emperor was told that some states, including Liu's State of Wu, were expanding their military strength, he adopted a number of steps to tighten control of the central government. After Liu's rebellion plot was brought to light, the Han emperor sent a large army to quash the revolt.

Three months later, all rebel troops in the State of Wu were wiped out and King Liu Pi, himself, was killed in a battle.

Today the popularity of the idiom *Wei Ru Lei Luan*—"precarious as a pile of eggs"—is largely due to the image it evokes rather than the mutiny that spawned it.

味 如 鸡 肋
wèi rú jī lèi

Chicken Ribs

Cao Cao, ruler of the Kingdom of Wei (AD 220-265), was not only a famous strategist and poet, but also the creator of a number of Chinese sayings which are still very popular today. One such expression is *Wei Ru Ji Lei* or "tastes like chicken ribs".

After several years of seesaw battles between the kingdoms of Wei and Shu in the Hanzhong area (today's Shaanxi Province), Cao decided to personally command a large army to launch a major

offensive against the enemy troops.

However, because the Shu had fortified their defence, Cao's attack was not as successful as expected.

During the following months, the two armies were locked in a demoralizing standoff. Meanwhile, provisions for the Cao troops were running out.

One evening, while Cao was having his supper, a general came in and asked Cao what would be the password for that night. Looking at the chicken rib soup on the table, Cao said: "Chicken ribs."

When Yang Xiu, a military adviser, was told the password, he immediately ordered his subordinates to start packing and get ready for withdrawal. The general was puzzled and asked Yang: "How do you know we are going to pull out?"

Yang said: "We've been in the stalemate for months. Tonight, the password named by the commander-in-chief was a signal of withdrawal.

"Chicken ribs give a good chew, but they are almost tasteless. We are now facing the same problem. The commander-in-chief is reluctant to pull out of the Hanzhong area, but it is certainly unconstructive and meaningless to stay any longer."

Yang's prediction was correct. The next morning, Cao ordered the withdrawal.

Today, the idiom *Wei Ru Ji Lei* is often used to describe anything that is of little value but would be a pity to throw away.

未 雨 绸 缪
wèi　　yǔ　　chóu　　móu

Before It Rains

Some Chinese expressions originated from popular verses. The idiom, *Wei Yu Chou Mou*, or "repair the house before it rains", is an example of just such a saying since it comes from a poem written by a politician some 3,000 years ago.

The Duke of Zhou, who was acting as regent when King Cheng of the Western Zhou Dynasty (11th century-771 BC) was still young, later left the imperial court and had to move out of the capital as rumours spread that he was trying to usurp the throne.

Living in de facto exile, the duke still cared, though, about state affairs and the well-being of the king. So, when he learned that two of the king's uncles were hatching a plot to stage a coup against the imperial court, he immediately wrote a poem and asked a friend to present it to the monarch.

In the poem, the duke told how a bird uses tree branches and leaves to repair its nest to prevent it from being destroyed by winds or rains.

One line in the poem reads: "Before it rains, I must repair the doors and windows with the roots of the white mulberry."

The warning contained in the poem was ignored by the king, who failed to take precautions against a possible coup.

It was not until the young ruler finally learned that the Duke of Zhou had been framed by his enemies that he decided to call the former regent back to help him foil the plot.

The duke's reinstatement was welcomed by both the court and the people. The rebellion that had been staged was soon put down and the regime of the Western Zhou was consolidated.

And the line in his poem about repairing the house later evolved into a widely-quoted saying.

Today, the idiom, *Wei Yu Chou Mou*, is used in persuading people to "save against a rainy day", "to take precautions" or "to provide for the future".

卧 薪 尝 胆

wò　　xīn　cháng　dǎn

Brushwood and Gall

One of the virtues most highly prized by the Chinese people is to show great patience or undergo great self-imposed hardships while achieving one's goals. This is particularly true when the goal is revenge.

So, the Chinese language has many popular sayings in praise of this attribute. The best known is perhaps the expression, *Wo Xin Chang Dan*, which means "to sleep on the brushwood and taste the gall".

This saying dates back to the late Spring and Autumn Period (770-476 BC), when during a war with the State of Wu, the king of the State of Yue was captured by the enemy. While captive, the king "swallowed his humiliation" and worked very hard as a horseman for the ruler of the State of Wu and as a result, three years later, he was released and allowed to go back to his home state.

After his return, though, the king refused to live in the palace. Instead, he fashioned a bed from a pile of brushwood in a dilapidated house where he then could hang a gallbladder from a pig from a string in the center of the hut.

Then each morning after he got up from his brushwood bed, and, then again, each evening before he went to bed, the king would taste of the bitter gall and then ask himself the question: "Have you forgotten the national humiliation?" He then would answer the same way each time: "No, I never will!"

The king had actually purposely designed this unpleasant lifestyle to make sure his determination for revenge became even more hardened. In the meantime, he was taking steps to carry out his vengeful plan. After recruiting a team of top-class advisers, he instituted a series of steps designed to improve the domestic economy and form a well-trained army. All the while, in order to lull his former captors into complacency, he kept sending a nearly continuous stream of luxurious gifts their way—beautiful women, priceless gems, fine horses and other luxuries. It took several years, but when the opportunity came, the Yue king launched an overall offensive and, within but a few days, the State of Wu was conquered.

Still today, the story of the Yue king's iron-clad determination and impressive self-restraint is told in almost every primary school classroom with admiration and the saying, *Wo Xin Chang Dan*, still is quoted in many a Chinese article, novel or play.

物 以 类 聚
wù　yǐ　lèi　jù

Birds of a Feather

"Birds of a feather flock together" is a popular phrase in English to describe how similar people will be found together.

In the Chinese language, there is a similar expression—*Wu Yi Lei Ju* or "Things of a kind come together". This phrase was created by a well-known Chinese scholar more than 2,000 years ago.

During the Warring States Period (475-221 BC), Chun Yukun of the Qi State enjoyed a high reputation for being a pedantic and eloquent academician. He often commented about state affairs in his lectures and speeches.

King Xuan of the State of Qi loved to be surrounded by talented people and famed scholars. One day, the king asked Chun Yukun whether he could find more talent around the state for the imperial court. Chun said that would be easy.

Next morning, the scholar brought seven "wise and able" persons to see the king. The monarch was very happy, but he wondered how could Chun find so many talented people in such a short time.

Therefore, he asked the scholar, "I was told that one would be lucky to find one wise and able person for every 1,000 square kilometres or find one sage every 100 years. So I'm surprised you could find seven persons of virtue for me in such a short time."

The scholar answered, "Your Majesty, it is true that it takes aeons to find dry crops in a wet and low-lying field, while you can find plenty of them on a plateau.

"Birds of the same type often fly together and animals of the same sort often are seen walking collectively. This means that things of a kind come together.

"Your Majesty came to me to seek talented people of my kind, so it is as easy as fetching water from a big river. Actually, I could bring more to see you in coming days."

Since then the scholar's illustration, *Wu Yi Lei Ju*, evolved into a popular idiom. Now it is also used in another popular Chinese saying, "Things of a kind come together, but people are divided into different groups".

相 煎 太 急
xiāng   jiān   tài   jí

Cooking Beans

Quarrels and killings among brothers are always tragic.

Such was the persecution of Cao Zhi, a famous writer in ancient China, by his own brother.

But this particular story did have one good result—the idiom *Xiang Jian Tai Ji*, still very popular in China today.

Cao Zhi was the fourth son of Cao Cao, the first ruler of the State of Wei during the Three Kingdoms Period (AD 220-280). One of

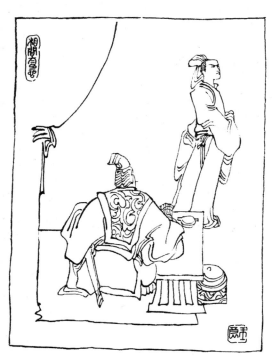

Cao Zhi's elder brothers was Cao Pi.

These three Caos, known in the history of Chinese literature as the "Cao Father and Sons", were all accomplished writers. But, of the three, Cao Zhi was by far the most talented.

As a teenager, Cao Zhi had already become a well-known writer. His father loved his fourth son very much and intended to name him his successor. But Cao Pi, though not the rival of his younger brother in writing, was much better at politics. He resorted to all kinds of schemes to squeeze Cao Zhi out of their father's favour and finally established himself as the heir to the throne.

After the father died and Cao Pi became ruler, the older brother persecuted Cao Zhi relentlessly. Although Cao Zhi had already lost his wife and many close friends, his brother still wanted him dead. It was only because of their mother's piteous, tearful entreaties that Cao Pi decided to give his younger brother one last chance.

One day, the new ruler summoned Cao Zhi to his presence and told him that he had violated some vital rule and must be executed.

"However, since you are my own brother," Cao Pi said, "I will give you an opportunity to survive on condition that you create a poem in the time it takes to walk no more than seven steps."

The younger brother replied, "Yes, I'll do it. Please name a topic."

Cao Pi said, "The topic is 'Brothers', but not once can the word 'brother' appear in the poem."

Before walking seven steps, Cao Zhi said aloud a poem to the effect, " 'A beanstalk is being used as the fuel to cook beans, and a bean is weeping in the pot.' Both of us have grown from the same root, so why are you now burning me in such haste?"

Hearing this poem, nearly everyone present was moved to tears, and even the elder brother felt sad and embarrassed.

Thanks to his talent, Cao Zhi escaped death that time, but because of continuous persecution and his deep depression, this highly gifted writer died at the age of only 41.

Soon after, the poem was on everybody's lips around the country, and the idiom *Xiang Jian Tai Ji*, or "burning beans in such haste", found its way into the catalogue of Chinese idioms.

Today, both Cao Zhi's poem about cooking beans and the idiom *Xiang Jian Tai Ji* are often used to describe fratricide or struggles among blood relatives.

胸 有 成 竹

xiōng　yǒu　chéng　zhú

Bamboo Painting

Like everywhere else in the world, to have a well-thought-out plan before embarking upon a new undertaking is deemed as wise and advisable among Chinese people. However, the Chinese tend to describe such wise and advisable practice in a quite unique and bizarre way. They say people who act according to well-prepared plans are those who have grown bamboo in their chests—*Xiong You Cheng Zhu*.

The idiom, *Xiong You Cheng Zhu*, was first used by people during the Northern Song Dynasty (AD 960-1126) to praise the exceptional artistry of the bamboo paintings created by Wen Tong, a well-known scholar at that time. Besides writing poems and practicing calligraphy, Wen loved painting bamboo most. He planted groves of bamboo all round his house and whenever he had time, he could be seen wandering in his "bamboo garden".

Year in and year out, careful observation had engraved in Wen's mind every graceful shape, nuance of colour, and detailed line of the plant. So, when he painted bamboo in his study, he painted according to the images formed in his mind instead of from direct observation. And the bamboo painted by Wen was so vivid and impressive that his art works were sought by other artists, scholars, government officials and rich merchants from all parts of the country.

Also, dozens of young artists came to visit Wen wishing that they could learn some of his superb skills in painting bamboo. While watching Wen painting bamboo, the young artists admired his knowledge and accomplishment, but could not quite understand how anyone could reach such perfection. So they turned to Wen's close friend, poet Chao Buzhi, for advice. Chao told them, "If you want to paint bamboo like Wen, you must have grown bamboo in your chests before you unfold the paper and pick up the brush."

Since then, *Xiong You Cheng Zhu* (with grown bamboo in the chest—literal translation) has been widely used to describe people who are well prepared for a new endeavor. So, next time you're going to carry out a plan, don't forget to grow bamboo in your chest first.

悬　梁　刺　股
xuán　liáng　cì　gǔ

Studying Hard

Chinese students are known for their hard work and self-discipline. This is but natural since the tradition of "studying assiduously" has been followed in China for more than 2,000 years. *Xuan Liang Ci Gu* is just one of a dozen idioms that are frequently cited today by parents and teachers in encouraging their children and young students to carry forward the fine tradition.

In fact, *Xuan Liang Ci Gu*, meaning "trying one's hair from a beam and pricking one's thigh with an awl" derives from two stories:

one about Su Qin, a famous strategist during the Warring States Period (475-221 BC), and the other involving Sun Jing, a learned scholar of the Western Han Dynasty (206 BC-AD 24).

Su's career as a strategist started with a total failure. He first went to serve the king of Qin, then a great power among seven ducal states which were fiercely vying with each other for hegemony in today's northern, eastern and central China. But the king had never accepted any of Su's ideas or proposals on how to conquer the other states.

Broken and depressed, Su retreated to his home in Luoyang, where he was ridiculed by his kinsmen and joked about even by his wife and sister-in-law. Su blamed his failure on his lack of knowledge of strategy and a thorough understanding of current affairs. Therefore, he decided to spend more time studying classical strategy.

Day and night, Su buried himself in books. Whenever he was too tired, he used an awl to prick his thigh to keep himself awake. More than 12 months later, the young strategist felt that he was well prepared and then set off for a new mission, this time to help the other six states to fight Qin.

Finally, Su helped form a chain of north-south alliances and he himself became the head of the so-called "Perpendicular Unionists", who advocated his policy of checking the growing power of Qin.

Sun Jing, before establishing himself as a learned scholar of the Western Han Dynasty, invented another way to keep himself awake while reading books during the night. He tied his hair to an overhead beam, so whenever he began to fall asleep, the painful yank of his hair invariably woke him up.

Fortunately, these self-tormenting schemes such as *Xuan Liang Ci Gu* are no longer practiced by Chinese students today.

However, the idiom has survived, and so has the tradition of "studying assiduously".

掩 耳 盗 铃

yǎn　ěr　dào　líng

Stealing a Bell

In English-speaking countries, people tend to describe a person who deceives himself and refuses to accept facts as burying his head in the sand like an ostrich. His counterpart in China, however, invented an easier way to achieve the same goal more than 2,000 years ago—to plug his ears while stealing a bell or *Yan Er Dao Ling*.

This Chinese idiom originates from a story that dates back to the Spring and Autumn Period (770-476 BC).

The Fan family was one of the large clans in the State of Jin. But the family was almost totally wiped out by its rivals.

One day, a man passed by the Fan's deserted house and saw a beautiful bronze bell still hanging above the front door. The man liked the bell very much and decided to steal it and take it home.

However, since the bell was so big and heavy, the thief found it impossible to take the whole bell home by himself. So, he planned to smash it into small pieces and carry the fragements home in a large bag.

First, the thief found a big harmmer and then, with all his might, he struck the bell. The bell cracked, but its deafening sound frightened the thief. He was afraid that the sound would attract the attention of people living in the neighbourhood and that he might be caught red-handed.

So the thief immediately plugged his ears and continued to smash at the bell, believing that as long as he could not hear the bell's sound, no one else would either.

By sheer chance or because of his tenacity, the thief was finally able to break the bell into small pieces without being seen.

It is probably due to this story *Yan Er Dao Ling* that today, one can not only frequently hear the idiom being cited in China, but also can find "bell swindlers" like the thief still roving about the country. Besides burying their heads in the sand, the Chinese ostriches also plug their ears.

叶　公　好　龙
shè　gōng　hào　lóng

Dragon Maniac

Probably everywhere around the world, you can find someone who praises the sea, but keeps to the land. In China, people tend to describe the phenomenon by quoting the popular idiom *She Gong Hao Long* or Lord She's love of the dragon.

Shen Zhuliang was only the magistrate of She in the State of Chu during the Spring and Autumn Period (770-476 BC). However, he insisted on others calling him "Lord She", who was best known for his infatuation with dragons.

The pendant on his robe was shaped like a dragon. The bowls and drinking cups in his house bore the design of dragons. And even the walls, columns, doors, windows, tables and chairs at his residence

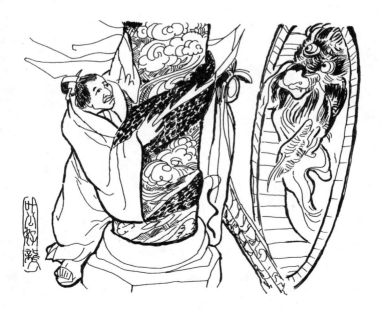

were all adorned with drawings and carvings of this legendary animal.

By learning all this, the real dragon in the Heaven was very much moved by Lord She's love of his kind. Therefore, the dragon decided to pay a visit to She's house.

One afternoon, when Lord She was taking a nap, the dragon arrived with deafening thunder and violent storms. The official awoke with a start. When he saw a real dragon poking its head in through the window and swinging its tail into the hall, he was frightened out of his wits and fainted.

Looking at the house which was fully decorated with drawings and carvings of dragons and the fainted man lying in the middle of it, the real dragon became puzzled. It was not until a while later that it began to dawn upon the "divine animal" that what Lord She really loved was something in the shape of a dragon, but not the real one.

Today, the idiom *She Gong Hao Long* is frequently cited to depict the professed love of what one really fears.

一　鸣　惊　人
yī　　míng　　jīng　　yén

The First Song

From time to time an obscure person may leap to fame with a single brilliant feat. In China, people tend to quote the idiom *Yi Ming Jing Ren* or "amazing the world with its first song" to describe anyone who sets the world on fire overnight.

In fact, this expression was first introduced by a king during the Warring States Period (475-221 BC).

King Wei of the State of Qi was enthroned when he was only in his 20s. The young ruler paid little mind to state affairs. Instead, he

played away the days and spent whole evenings drinking. For three consecutive years, his ministers had rarely seen the king holding court.

As a result, the political and economic situation in the state kept deteriorating. And several neighbouring states had begun to invade its border areas.

Some patriotic court officials were deeply worried about the future of the state. Therefore, they asked Chunyu Kun, a silver-tongued politician, to warn the young ruler over the possible collapse of the State of Qi.

Chunyu knew that the king liked subtlety in language. So, one day he came to see the king and told him a story.

He said that there was a bird perching on a tree near the imperial court. For three years, it had never fluttered its wings or uttered a sound. "Does Your Highness know what's wrong with that bird?"

The king immediately saw the point of the story. He answered: "I know the bird. Should it desire to fly, it would soar into the sky with great flourish, and should it desire to sing, it would amaze the world with its first song."

Next morning, by pushing aside his concubines and maids of honour and kicking away his wine cups, the king came into the court.

He summoned the 72 magistrates of the state to his presence. Then, he honored one magistrate for his excellent performance and executed another for neglect of his trusted duties.

In the following months, the king personally led the royal armies to repel the invaders. After winning the border wars, the king began to concentrate on boosting agricultural production in the state.

Thanks to the arduous efforts of the king and his aides, the State of Qi remained a strong power for the next 36 years.

Nowadays, the idiom *Yi Ming Jing Ren* is often cited to make note of a person who amazes the world with his first work. It is also used as a compliment to anyone who has made a success in his career with a single accomplishment.

一 诺 千 金
yī　nuò　qiān　jīn

Golden Promise

A trustworthy person must be one who is true to his words. The Chinese show great respect for such people and have preserved in their language the idiom *Yi Nuo Qian Jin* to describe anyone whose "promise is weightier than one thousand taels of gold".

This idiom originates from a story about Ji Bu, a well-known chief officer of the imperial bodyguards in the court of the Western Han Dynasty (206BC-AD24).

Ji was born and brought up in the Chu area in eastern China. Known as a master of martial arts and advocate of personal honour and loyalty, Ji joined the rebel army fighting against the rule of the

Qin Dynasty (221-206 BC) when he was only in his early twenties.

After the collapse of the Qin regime, Ji became a chief officer of the imperial bodyguards of the newly-established Western Han Dynasty after narrowly surviving some political persecution cases against him.

However, despite the change in his position and personal experience of career setbacks, Ji remained an outspoken critic of things he disliked.

One day, he openly advised his friends to distance themselves from Cao Qiusheng, a smooth-tongued aide in the court whom Ji despised.

After learning Ji's comments, Cao came to see the chief officer of the imperial bodyguards and asked to have a talk with him.

Cao said: "You are widely reputed as a trustworthy person. This is largely due to the fact that in the Chu area, everyone says that 'A promise made by Ji Bu is weightier than one thousand taels of gold.'

"I am from the Chu area, too. But, I cannot understand what makes me such a loathsome person in your eyes."

Cao's flattery gradually melted away the mistrust between the two imperial aides. Later, they became good friends. Since then, the silver-tongued Cao tried his best to beautify the image and reputation of Ji Bu.

Obviously, Cao's efforts have proved to be very successful. Even today, many Chinese have learned about the name of Ji Bu through the idiom *Yi Nuo Qian Jin*, created by Cao more than 2,000 years ago.

一　丘　之　貉
yī　qiū　zhī　hé

Jackals from the Same Lair

Yi Qiu Zhi He (meaning, "jackals from the same lair") could be considered one of the most deadly expressions of the Chinese language, since it meant death to the outspoken official who first used the phrase some 20 centuries ago.

Yang Yun was a high-ranking aide to Emperor Xuan of the Western Han Dynasty. He believed in clean government and was known as one of the few truly impartial and incorruptible officials of the time. But he also had made many enemies because of his caustic manner and his relentless passion to bring court scandals to

light.

One day while he was riding through the streets with some of his colleagues, a horse suddenly shied and galloped out of the northern city gates. Yang commented, "The last time a horse shied and ran into a city gate, it was just several days until Emperor Zhao died. Maybe today's incident also is a harbinger from above."

When Emperor Xuan heard about Yang's remarks, he was very unhappy, but the outspoken official was not about to be silenced.

A few months later, when Yang learned that a Hun tribal chieftain had killed himself because he was opposed by his people for they hated his tyrannical rule, he said publicly: "Unpopular rulers who refuse to listen to be criticism and suggestions made by upright officials are bound to die in disgrace. Such autocratic rulers are jackals from the same lair."

His remarks were taken to be a direct attack on the imperial court and the emperor, so the emperor decided that Yang must be punished. At first, he relieved Yang of all his posts and expelled him from the court. As young continued to condemn the court's practices, Emperor Xuan decided to have him executed.

Today, the expression *Yi Qiu Zhi He* is used by Chinese-speakers in a much the same way as the English expressions, "birds of a feather" or "tigers from the same den" are used, except the Chinese saying has an uneqivocally derogatory connotation.

一 叶 障 目
yī　yè　zhàng　mù

A Magic Leaf

Probably many young children or even adults have once in their lives dreamed of having a magic cloak or stick that will make them invisible whenever they choose.

The Chinese idiom *Yi Ye Zhang Mu*, "blocking one's view by a leaf", indicates such a dream began to haunt people aeons ago.

This idiom is based on a story about a poor scholar who lived in the State of Chu in eastern China thousands of years ago. For many years, he and his wife led a miserable life.

The poor scholar was a typical daydreamer who could neither do hard labour in the fields or climb the social echelons. But, he believed he was destined to become rich someday.

One day, he came across a paragraph in a book which said if one obtained the leaf under which a mantis hides itself before preying on a cicada, he would be able to become invisible by blocking his eyes with the leaf. The scholar was overjoyed by this discovery.

For the next few days, he wandered around the village searching for such a leaf. Finally, he found one.

To see whether it worked, the scholar first used the leaf to cover his left eye and asked his wife if she could see him. The wife said yes. Then, he used the leaf to cover his right eye and asked his wife the same question. Again, the wife said that she could see him.

The scholar did not intend to give up, so he tried again and again and repeatedly asked his wife the same question. Eventually, his wife was fed up with the game and answered that she could no longer see him.

The scholar thought the magic leaf had begun to work. So, the next day he went to a market and stole goods from a vendor by blocking his own eye with the leaf.

He was immediately caught and brought to the local magistrate. The official asked the scholar how could he dare to take other people's properties in broad daylight. The scholar told the magistrate the story about the magic leaf.

After hearing the story, the official burst into laughter and then he let the scholar go unpunished. The magistrate told others: "That poor guy must be a nut."

Today, the idiom *Yi Ye Zhang Mu* is still very popular among Chinese. Maybe, this is because there are still so many "nuts" around who tend to have their view of the important overshadowed by the trival.

饮 鸩 止 渴
yǐn   zhèn   zhǐ   kě

Poisoned Wine

In a desperate situation, people tend to seek temporary relief regardless of the consequences. Chinese speakers will quote the saying *Yin Zhen Zhi Ke* or "drinking poisoned wine to quench your thirst" to describe such an act.

The Chinese character for *Zhen* that is used in the expression is the name of a legendary bird which has purplish green feathers and

likes to eat snakes.

It is said that the Zhen's feathers are deadly poisonous. In ancient times, people sometimes put a Zhen feather into wine to make it toxic.

The Chinese phrase that refers to the drinking of Zhen wine was first cited by Huo Xu, an official of the Eastern Han Dynasty (AD 25-220).

When Huo was only 15, his uncle, Song Guang, was accused of rewriting a document issued by the imperial court without authorization.

To defend his jailed uncle, the teenager wrote a letter to a general in charge of the case.

In the letter, Huo said that his uncle was an honest man and upright official.

"Also, he is a very cautious person who would not do things like drinking Zhen wine just to quench his thirst," Huo said in the letter. "Therefore, it can't be possible for Uncle Song Guang to have made changes in the imperial document for personal interests or any other reason."

The general was impressed by the teenager's letter and personally attended the hearings on the case. Huo eventually managed to help clear his uncle's name and some years later himself became a high-ranking official of the imperial court.

Today, the idiom *Yin Zhen Zhi Ke* is used to persuade people not to seek any sort of temporary relief which will result in disaster.

游 刃 有 余
yóu　rèn　yǒu　yú

A Butcher's Cleaver

Ancient Chinese people held in great respect anyone who was armed with consummate skills in his special field, no matter whether he was a carpenter, tailor, painter, calligrapher, thief, cook or butcher. Many stories and idioms about such masters are still quite

popular in China today. The idiom *You Ren You Yu* or "There is plenty of room for a butcher's cleaver" is but one of them.

During the Warring States Period (475-221 BC), there was a butcher in the State of Wei who enjoyed a high reputation for his unique skills in butchering cattle. The duke of the State of Wei intended to offer the butcher a job in the royal kitchen. So, one day, the duke invited the butcher to perform his skill in the presence of an audience, including the duke himself.

The butcher first slaughtered an ox in a manner little different from what an ordinary butcher would do and the slow process almost put the audience to sleep.

After hanging the dressed body of the ox on a big pole, the butcher began to cut the carcass into pieces. He used his shoulders, knees and feet to hold the carcass steady. Then, in just a split second and with a few lightning movements of his cleaver, the butcher cut the carcass into a dozen pieces of almost exactly the same size.

The audience was first dumfounded by the dazzling performance and then burst into a prolonged round of loud applause.

The butcher told the duke that when he first entered the business, he saw the carcass as a whole and did not know where to start cutting it. Three years later, after having carefully studied the structure of the cattle skeleton, he could see every joint and every piece of bone in a carcass with just one glance.

The master butcher said that an ordinary butcher would have to change his cleaver every month because he used it to cut the bones; and a skillful butcher would have to change his cleaver every year because he used it to cut the carcass meat.

"Now, the cleaver in my hand has been used by me for 19 years and I have never ground it since I bought it. But, you can see it is still as sharp as a brand-new one. This is because I can find plenty of room in a carcass for maneuvering my cleaver," the butcher explained.

Nowadays, people cite the idiom *You Ren You Yu* to describe anyone who can do a job with skill and ease or who is more than equal to his task.

愚 公 移 山
yú   gōng   yí   shān

Foolish Old Man

In China, Yu Gong (the Foolish Old Man) is a character familiar to everyone. The legendary hero not only appears in primary school textbooks, but also helps to personify determination in political slogans such as "to transform China in the spirit of the Foolish Old Man".

According to legend, there was an old man, called the Foolish Old Man, living in Jizhou, North China, a long, long time ago. In front of the old man's house were two high mountains, one called Taihang

Mountain and the other Wangwu Mountain. The two blocked the way to Yuzhou and Hanshui, the two nearest towns. To visit the towns, the old man and his family had to take long detours or climb over the high mountains.

One day, the old man called a meeting of his whole family and announced a plan to move the two mountains. His proposal was readily accepted by all members of the family. Only the old man's wife hesitantly asked: "Where can we dispose of the immense amount of earth and stones?" One of her grandchildren immediately answered: "Don't worry, Grandma. We can throw them into the Bohai Sea."

So, the next morning, the whole family went to dig up the two mountains. Soon, some of the old man's neighbours joined the family, bringing their own tools. Day and night, rain or shine, they worked very hard and never stopped digging.

One day, another grey-beard, called Zhisou (the Wise Old Man), came by the site and asked the Foolish Old Man: "Aren't you silly? At your age and with such a small group of people, do you think you can ever clear away the two mountains?"

The Foolish Old Man replied: "Why not? I may not live long enough to see the two mountains moved from here. But after I die, my sons will carry on the project. After my sons die, my grandchildren will continue to dig up the mountains. And my grandchildren will have their own sons and grandchildren. At the same time, the two mountains are not likely to grow any higher. So as long as we keep digging, why can't the two mountains be cleared away someday?"

Hearing his remarks, God was moved by the firm determination of the Foolish Old Man. One night, he sent down two angels, who carried away the two mountains on their backs.

鹬 蚌 相 争
yù　　bàng　　xiāng　　zhēng

Snipe and Clam

In ancient times, many Chinese politicians were good at creating thought-provoking stories to illustrate their arguements. Some of these stories later became popular Chinese idioms.

Yu Bang Xiang Zheng, Yu Weng De Li—or "When the snipe and the clam grapple, the fisherman profits"—is a good example.

During the Warring States Period (475-221 BC), the State of Zhao planned to launch a military offensive against the State of

Yan. The two states were quarreling over some trivial problems. After learning about the plan, a man named Su Dai from Luoyang, the ancient city in today's Henan Province, paid a visit to the State of Zhao in an attempt to persuade the Duke of Zhao to cancel the move.

Instead of going directly to the point, Su first told the duke a story. "On my way here, I saw a snipe grappling with a clam near the Yishui River," Su said. "The bird's long beak was locked shut by the clam. The snipe told the clam that it would just wait until the clam dried up and died, but the clam replied that it would not let go of the bird's beak until the snipe starved to death. When the two were nearly exhausted, a passing fisherman caught them both."

Then Su told the Duke of Zhao that the State of Zhao and the State of Yan were equal in military strength, so that a war between the two would damage both, without either turning out to be the winner. Meanwhile, the State of Qin, a neighbouring superpower, might benefit from the dispute. Therefore, Su said, it was in the State of Zhao's own interest to call off the planned military move against the State of Yan.

The Duke of Zhao was convinced and he immediately cancelled the military plan. The duke said, "I believe there is truth in the story that Su has just told me."

朝 三 暮 四
zhāo　sān　mù　sì

Monkey's Nature

In English, people use adjectives such as "capricious", "wayward" and "arbitrary" to describe anyone who is erratic and changeable. Such persons also remind one of phrases including "blowing hot and cold" and "playing fast and loose". But in Chinese, we tend to label changeable persons with the popular idiom *Zhao San Mu Si*, or three in the morning and four in the evening.

Originally, the story behind this Chinese idiom did not concern man but his primate cousin—the monkey. The story goes like this:

During the Warring States Period (475-221 BC), there was an old

man called Ju Gong living in the State of Song. The old man loved monkeys. So he raised a large group of the primates near his home and, every day, he spent most of his time with his pets.

Gradually, Ju Gong began to know the psychology of the monkeys and the latter began to understand their master's language. So they could communicate with each other in a special way, and the old man and the monkeys all had many good times together.

But the monkeys were big eaters. Although Ju Gong tried hard to save as much food as possible from the mouths of his own family for his pets' sake, he still could not find enough to feed them. Therefore, one morning, the old man came to discuss the food shortage problem with the monkeys.

Since he knew that his pets would not be happy about food rationing, he decided to take advantage of the psychological characteristics of the monkeys to trick them into accepting his plan. The old man told the monkeys: "Starting today, I will feed each of you three acorns in the morning and four in the evening. Is that enough?"

With angry expressions on their faces, the monkeys jumped wildly around their master in protest against the cut in food supply. Then Ju Gong said: "Okay, okay. I'll give you four acorns in the morning and three in the evening. Does that satisfy your mischievous creatures?"

The monkeys thought the old man had raised the food ration and became very happy. Imitating what ancient people did, the monkeys kowtowed to the old man to express their gratitude.

So when the idiom of *Zhao San Mu Si* first found its way into the Chinese language, it was used to describe someone employing tricks to cheat others. Later on, however, it gained a new meaning of "being capricious and changeable". Today, the idiom is always cited in accordance with its new meaning and few remember its original definition.

纵 虎 归 山
zòng　hǔ　guī　shān

Let the Tiger Escape

Chinese devotees to Buddha believe that it's a philanthropic act to free captive animals. Therefore, during important Buddhist festivals, they often buy captive fish or birds and set them free.

However, not all animals are suitable for this purpose. For instance, few Chinese people believe in *Zong Hu Gui Shan* or "let the tiger return to the mountain".

This popular Chinese saying, comes from a story about Liu Bei, a hero during the Three Kingdoms period (AD 220-280).

During the late years of the Eastern Han Dynasty (AD 25-220),

China was rushed into an overall civil war. One day, Liu Bei went to Cao Cao—who later became the ruler of the Wei Kingdom—for protection after being defeated by another warlord.

One of Cao's advisers told him that Liu was an ambitious man who could become a rival and block Cao's plan for unifying the country in the future. So, the adviser repeatedly tried to persuade Cao to kill him.

But Cao refused to do so. He said it was time to invite to his side men of wisdom and valour instead of persecuting able and virtuous persons.

Cao showed great hospitality and respect to Liu while the latter tried his best to hide his ambitions and ostentatiously demonstrated his modesty.

One day, Liu told Cao that he was willing to lead an army to attack the invading enemy. Cao agreed.

After learning the news, the suspicious adviser immediately asked for the permission to see Cao. He told Cao that it would be very wrong to let Liu go.

"This is like freeing a dragon to the sea and allowing a tiger to return to the mountain," said the adviser.

"It could lead to serious problems in the future, so you'd better order Liu to bring back the troops right now."

It was already too late, though, and Liu refused to obey the new order from Cao. He left the territory controlled by Cao troops and eventually set up his own kingdom, and did thus become one of Cao's chief rivals.

The metaphor used by that adviser has today evolved into a popular idiom. *Zong Hu Gui Shan* is now frequently cited by Chinese speakers to describe any decision which may cause calamity for future.